HARMONY IN WORSHIP

Building supportive relationships between clergy, musicians and congregations

STEPHEN MITCHELL
ROGER GREEN

kevin mayhew

kevin
mayhew

First published in Great Britain in 2016 by Kevin Mayhew Ltd
Buxhall, Stowmarket, Suffolk IP14 3BW
Tel: +44 (0) 1449 737978 Fax: +44 (0) 1449 737834
E-mail: info@kevinmayhew.com

www.kevinmayhew.com

9 8 7 6 5 4 3 2 1 0

ISBN 978 1 84867 860 6
Catalogue No. 1501530

Cover design by Rob Mortonson
© Image used under licence from Shutterstock Inc.
Edited by Nicki Copeland
Typeset by Angela Selfe

Printed and bound in Great Britain

Contents

About the authors

Stephen Mitchell studied music at Exeter University where he was the Organ Scholar and Chapel choirmaster before teaching music in a secondary school. After ordination and a curacy at Malvern Priory, he was appointed Precentor at Leicester Cathedral and head of RE at Leicester Grammar School. He has recently retired after nearly forty years in the ministry during which he continued to make music and run a benefice choir.

Roger Green studied at Trinity College, London, and the Universities of Wales and Reading. He studied organ with Martindale Sidwell and became an organist and choirmaster at the age of 15. He has held posts in several churches while following a teaching career in a variety of establishments, retiring from the University of Cambridge. He currently plays regularly in two churches and deputises in others.

Prelude

Perhaps you are standing in a shop and have just picked up this book. This is the bit you might read before purchasing it. It is rather like the music before the service begins. Whether you liked it or not, it started you thinking and you stayed to see if anything else would continue to stimulate those thoughts.

No two churches, no two organists, no two choirs, no two worship bands, no two clergy are the same. What works for one will not work for another. There are few off-the-shelf answers, but there are questions that can provoke discussion and shed light.

In the spirit of encouraging dialogue between musicians and clergy we have included in the book a number of question sections. We hope these might stimulate thought and conversation and, where appropriate, lead to joint action. In exploring the questions we hope that musicians and clergy may be able to discover strategies that will be beneficial in their particular circumstances.

You will find many quotations in this book. Many have welcomed the opportunity to share their views. The sources are not cited, and that is because we have promised that the views expressed will not be attributable. Any names and locations have been changed. All the quotations are 'as offered' by members of the clergy, congregation or musicians who work in church. We include them because they illustrate the range of beliefs and experiences of those who have week-to-week contact with church music.

> 'If they sing it well, it transforms the service.'
>
> 'It doesn't matter what the music is, if it is of quality.'
>
> 'If you are going to have music in church, you have to make sure that it is done well.'
>
> 'If you have a decent organist or decent music group, it is the best advertisement for the church.'

Perhaps that is your experience. Perhaps your congregation is accustomed to high quality in terms of the music and in terms of the liturgy.

Surprisingly, the next two quotations come from clergy:

> 'Why are there so many sloppy priests?'
>
> 'I do not know why so many of the clergy are so dictatorial.'

Some clergy seem to feel under threat from their resident musician or musicians. Several members of the clergy told us:

> 'There should be a musical component in clergy training.'

Certainly a conviction that, as a member of the clergy, you do not really understand what music is all about, and that the agenda of the musicians in your church might be different from yours, can lead to mistrust and conflict between clergy and musicians. Not all clergy hold musicians in high regard, and sadly 'twas ever so.

> 'The devil has a technique of finding a way into worship – often through the organ or organist.'
>
> 'There are two kinds of organists: the first would be in church anyway and the second would not darken the doors if they were not playing.'
>
> 'I know full well that he doesn't believe but his music speaks eloquently to those who do.'

So some musicians, like some bell-ringers, would not own up to a religious faith. That too is probably not a new thing. In William Byrd's day the divide was between Protestant and Catholic belief. Today it is between belief and non-belief, and both come in many shades. Many church musicians would tell you that they are humanists. Some would tell you that they are atheists. At the same time, many of those musicians create music of great beauty – music that has the power to transform. And many of them are devoted to the music of the church. Andrew Gant says:

> 'And where is faith? Is it possible for a musician to create church music without being a believer? Manifestly, it is. Most leading composers of church music of the last hundred years have not been conventional believers.'[1]

All the same, it is probably at least slightly unnerving for the minister or priest to know that a key member of the team that is making worship possible does not subscribe to what they might well view as the purpose of the worship.

> 'It must offer a glimpse of heaven.'
>
> 'It must create a moving experience.'
>
> 'Can we begin to know that music can speak about otherness?'
>
> 'Can we be daring enough to use music to find the silences?'

What is it in our services that speaks to us and to the congregation? It will not be the same for all.

---

1. Andrew Gant, *O Sing unto the Lord* (London: Profile Books Ltd, 2015), p.375.

> 'Have you ever asked, as they file out, what has spoken to them?'
>
> 'They never stop telling me what was wrong with it, but they seldom seem to share what moved them.'

A comparison between what we do in church services and a performance is instructive. In worship there are many elements of musical and dramatic performance. Like all performance, if it is to be effective it must all be of the highest quality that we can manage in our particular setting. That setting might vary from a packed cathedral to a small chapel 'where two or three are gathered together'. But if you disagree that quality is paramount, you might as well not read any more.

> 'You have to realise that you are developing a performance.'
>
> 'I sometimes wonder, why not have the courage to invite a theatrical director to look at our service and direct it as a performance? We might learn significantly.'

And it is more than the words and the music; it is the whole effect.

> 'A few weeks ago I stopped to think. I've got this wonderful church building. It was made to speak to the people. And am I using the building in any way creatively?'

Both musicians and clergy have a role to play. If the music is offered in a careless, casual or unconvincing way, why should the delivery of the liturgy be any better? Or as one priest told us:

> 'If you are not taking care over the liturgy, why hammer the organist?'

If you have ever been involved in a business, you will know that the most exciting outcomes do not arise from talking down your business. Yet those involved in what happens in church might be forgiven for believing that talking down worship and being apologetic about it is perfectly acceptable.

> 'We are inviting people to invest in a closing-down sale.'
>
> 'Are we at the stage of inviting people to buy shares in Woolworths?'
>
> 'Should we necessarily be interested in full churches? Perhaps live, vibrant churches, even if the congregation is small, should interest us. You won't get "live and vibrant" by moaning about numbers or moaning about anything else.'

Vibrant churches can be the heart of the community. They are at the centre of things, just like the church is supposed to be. People meet their neighbours, they know members of their community, and they trust them and relate to them.

> 'The church must be a powerhouse for the community.'

> 'Our village hall was on the brink of collapse so we took the pews out of the nave of the church and made it available to the community.'

So if you are to focus on quality, and if your church is to be bursting with life, you may be thinking that a mini-cathedral in every town and village is required. The key, however, is to find liturgy and music to suit each place of worship. And that searching process is something that clergy and musicians should enter into together.

> 'In the town, St ________ does the music so the others need not.'

> 'In the benefice we do different musical styles in the different churches.'

And that takes us back to the point from which we started. No two churches, no two organists, no two choirs, no two worship bands, no two clergy are the same. What works for one will not work for another. There are few off-the-shelf answers, but there are questions that can provoke discussion and shed light.

We hope that by now you have decided to buy the book.

ONE

Music in worship

Worship

Christians of all denominations are called to worship. The psalmist calls us to 'Worship the Lord with gladness; come into his presence with singing' (Psalm 100:2). In his letter, the apostle Peter encourages us to worship because of who we are: 'But you are a chosen race, a royal priesthood, a holy nation, God's own people, in order that you may proclaim the mighty acts of him who called you out of darkness into his marvellous light' (1 Peter 2:9).

And how are we to worship? The writer to the Hebrews tells us: 'Therefore, since we are receiving a kingdom that cannot be shaken, let us give thanks, by which we offer to God an acceptable worship with reverence and awe; for indeed our God is a consuming fire' (Hebrews 12:28, 29). Jesus himself, in conversation with a Samaritan woman at Jacob's well, offered some instructions: 'God is spirit, and those who worship him must worship in spirit and truth' (John 4:24).

What must surely strike the musician, as well as all those responsible for worship, from these few verses is that worship is to be vital and imaginative. There is to be joy and gladness, reverence and awe, and a reflection of our transformation from darkness to light inspired by an awareness of the consuming fire of God and his Spirit.

Oxford theologian John Macquarrie once spoke about life in the Spirit as life in the 'imagination of God'. If ever there is a failure in our worship, it is often a failure of the imagination. From the beginning, Christians have used their imagination in the design and decoration of their churches; in the writing of prayers and in the creation of stained-glass windows, stone statues and wooden carvings; in embroidering vestments and arranging flowers. Whether the results are a rich tapestry of sound, light and colour or the simplest and plainest of devotions, worship is a drama carefully crafted.

No one directs a play without giving thought to the staging and costumes. A film is produced only after the musical score has been neatly tailored to the pace and action. A service of worship should be collaboratively planned with the same care and attention to detail, even though such planning may give rise to logistical problems in drawing people together. Some would rely on the workings of the Holy Spirit. Some would offer the thought that the workings of the Holy Spirit might benefit from people meeting and talking and listening.

If we are using liturgies from the past, we inherit patterns of worship moulded by centuries of thought. Even so, the onus is on us, as it would be with a play by Shakespeare, to understand the reasons why various elements take a particular form and to present them in a fresh and meaningful way. If we are creating a new service, the need for partnership between all those contributing to the worship is just as great.

Performance is only one aspect of worship. Our word 'worship' carries with it the meaning of worthiness and ascribing worth. The words in the Bible translated as 'worship' have other connotations. Some allude to the service being offered and the work and sacrifice involved. The word 'liturgy' literally means 'the work of the people'. Other words translated as 'worship' refer to a posture of submission and reverence. Worship forms our response to the God in whom we live and move and have our being. It is our duty and our joy.

> 'True worship is looking upon God, concentrating our whole being – minds, eyes, ears, emotions, wills – upon his presence, thereby offering him our best and laying ourselves open to his transforming grace.'

Throughout the history of Christianity there have been conflicting views on the effectiveness of music in worship. The Bible encourages the use of music, and many have recognised the emotional power of music to move the spirit. At the same time there have been those who have mistrusted that power and have sought to exclude music from worship. Quakers traditionally find no place for music in their worship, and some who read this book may well have been deeply moved while attending a Quaker service in spite of the absence of music.

Following the biblical example, other denominations have worked to harness the power of music to the benefit of all the worshippers. Puritans, Lutherans, Evangelicals and Tractarians have encouraged their congregations to sing wholeheartedly as part of worship. The meeting of text and music has been a frequent cause of debate as many have sought to advocate that the two should make a perfect marriage. Agreement, however, concerning the nature of a perfect marriage has been more elusive.

On the other hand, there have been those, particularly in the eighteenth and nineteenth centuries, for whom music of the highest quality has been valued as a vital part of the act of worship. This view has often led to an insistence on a performance by professional musicians, both singers and instrumentalists. We are justifiably proud of the high standard of music making in our cathedrals, even though at times this has been variable – notably in the early nineteenth century when musical standards in many places slipped drastically: the choir at St Paul's Cathedral, for example, was reduced to six members.

These two views have led to disagreement over the nature of music in worship. Is it about the musical inclusiveness enabling the congregation to take an active part, or is it about furnishing music of the highest quality and probably therefore reliant on professional musicians? Over the centuries there has been a tendency for musicians to enrich and embellish music, thus increasing the complexity to a point where those with less musical training can find it difficult to take part or perhaps even comprehend what they are hearing. There have been moments when attempts have been made to arrest this process, from the time of the Council of Trent, through Cranmer, Calvin and on to Pope John XXII.

What is worship?

Any discussion in our churches should start at the very heart of the matter with a series of questions that might take us towards an agreed understanding of the meaning of worship. That meaning will be different for each of us.

Questions for discussion

- Why do we worship?
- Is worship merely cultural conditioning?
- Is worship a truly collective experience?
- Who is worship for?
- Is it for the already faithful?
- Is it for those who have not 'signed up' (yet)?
- Do you always remember why you are worshipping?

And, returning to our thoughts in the previous section, we could ask . . .

- Whatever we do in worship, should it not be done to the highest standards?
- What variety of impressions will different readers of this book form from the words 'highest standards'?
- What factors might determine those 'highest standards'?
- How would you, as a musician, priest or minister, resolve these issues in your particular situation?

We might also spend some moments thinking about whether it is possible to work to the highest standards and still have the interests of the average worshipper in mind.

> 'We have a variety of services in the month and the music varies greatly between them. Sometimes we use the organ; sometimes a worship group with guitars, drums and other instruments.'

> 'We have tried some services that are outside our normal experience. They appeal to different people.'
>
> 'We have a service using Taizé music and chants about four times a year.'

You may have been regaled by a friend who describes their discomfort at attending a service in a church with which they were unfamiliar. What caused the friend to experience discomfort was the very thing that you felt was essential.

> 'I've known some worshippers go out complaining bitterly, while others wax lyrical at the same hymns. I often feel that the two groups should speak to one another about their contrasting reaction.'

Let us consider one Anglican church. There is a communion service early on Sunday mornings. This is a spoken service without music. There is a faithful but small band of parishioners who turn up most weeks because that service suits their needs. Slightly later there is a Eucharist service with music and a congregation averaging about 100 in number. Members of the congregation are encouraged to undertake active roles within the service. The age range is fairly broad, and six or seven children leave for part of the service to have their own activities. In the afternoon, once a month, there is a service of Choral Evensong. Just a few of those who have worshipped in the morning attend this, which is essentially a service based around the choir. Congregations tend to match those numbers attending the early communion service, but fewer are local and some are tourists.

Each of those services has its own distinct identity. With the exception of the organist, choir and clergy, those attending also have a distinct identity, and there is not much overlap between them. A particular service attracts particular worshippers because they prefer to worship in a way in which they feel comfortable.

Neither the organist nor the majority of the choir attend the spoken service. Most of the choir and the organist attend the Eucharist. The choir feel that they have a role in leading the singing, and the organist has reservations about some of the hymns that are chosen by the clergy. There is also a tension between priest and organist related to the congregational setting most often used in this service. All the choir members attend the Choral Evensong, and the organist knows that the majority of time at choir practices is spent in learning and perfecting the settings to the canticles, the pointing of the psalms, the anthem and the responses. The organist also believes that some of his choir would lose interest and melt away without the challenge of this monthly service.

What is the justification for each service? Perhaps the organist believes he knows. Perhaps the priest believes he knows. The agenda for the Eucharist is largely set by the priest and that for Evensong by the organist. The organist will have agreed, some while ago, to the priest's request for the introduction of a congregational hymn into the pattern for Evensong. Strangely, they don't seem to have talked about it.

Three very different forms of worship live within one parish church, but if we look on a wider canvas at the other churches in the town the picture is even more varied. All these varied forms have developed over years and are still developing to meet the worshipping needs of the inhabitants of the town. Whole new churches have sprung up, and are still springing up, to serve the needs of new groups of worshippers.

What is the role of music in worship?

A further fundamental question in any church's discussion will be about its understanding of the role of music in worship.

Some will wish to focus on the power of music to speak in its own language.

> 'When words fail, music does not.'
>
> 'I believe that music can take us to God when words seem inadequate.'
>
> 'I believe that music can be so powerful in worship.'
>
> 'Not many people would claim that music has not touched them in some way.'
>
> 'Music has to be there to help people to worship.'
>
> 'I believe that there is a case to be made for some services not needing music.'
>
> 'Music in church is boring.'

Some will wish to focus on the power of music to reinforce the collective nature of worship.

> 'A live musical performance is a collective social experience.'

Some will be set in their ways, believing that they know what will be effective in worship in their church.

> 'The music performed by our organist goes right over the heads of the congregation but she does not seem to notice.'
>
> 'The organist refuses to change.'
>
> 'The new minister does not seem to see any point in music being part of worship.'
>
> 'The minister only wants his style of hymns.'

Two elements will underpin most discussions. The first will concern what is available to make the music. The second will be about the kind of music to be made.

> 'There are two problems associated with music in worship. The first is related to resources and skills. The second is related to style and preference.'

Despite many complaints being levelled against music and musicians, music has been an important part of worship since at least the time of King David. Where problems and criticisms have arisen they have often been caused by musical preference or style, and that seems still to be true today. You will have met clergy and musicians who claim to represent the musical preference of the worshippers in their church. How sound that claim is in reality should be a point for investigation, especially when the views of clergy and musicians differ, with each claiming a view based on the same group of worshippers.

Many would agree that music, in some form, is essential to the human spirit. If you believe that music can affect or move people, you might care to ask yourself some questions which could form a basis for discussion between clergy and musicians in your church.

Questions for discussion

- Why is music important to you?
- Why is music important in your church?
- How can you ensure that the music is always 'done well'?
- What complaints are sometimes voiced against the music or musicians in your church?
- Why is music under threat in some churches?
- How does that threat relate to resources?
- How does that threat relate to skills?
- How does that threat relate to musical preferences?
- How can you be informed about the musical preferences of those who worship in your church?
- If those preferences are split, how can they be reconciled?
- How does that threat relate to musical style?
- How can you be confident that your musical style is the style with which the congregation might feel at home?
- What positive outcomes might result from challenging the style preferences of some?
- What differences would it make if you had to have a service without music?

Setting the mood

A sense of reverence and awe will form some part of our worship, and many will feel that music can help to create such an atmosphere or mood. Some musicians and clergy will not be conscious of using music in this role, and to some of those it might be a useful stimulus to thought. One person tells us that 'when words fail, music does not'. Another offers the thought that 'music can take us to God when words seem inadequate'. We admit to contemplating, from time to time, whether a musical performance might have taken the worshippers to God more effectively than the sermon to which we are trying to listen.

Music may well be an important factor in helping to create mood in your worship. If not, perhaps it would be worthwhile giving some thought as to how that might be achieved.

We might sometimes wonder at the number of words expended in a service. We have sometimes marvelled at the ability of some to tell us what we are going to do, tell us what we are doing and then tell us what we have done!

Yet sometimes words can assist music in creating a mood. Words can be spoken with a gentle musical accompaniment. That practice is relatively rare. Perhaps you have tried using music as an accompaniment to spoken words in your services.

> 'I often like to speak a prayer over music – say at the offertory – which means that there is no break in the music being offered.'

So much of our life is accompanied by music. We love our car radios and our headphones. Strange then, perhaps, that so few instances of music being used as a background in the context of a service spring to mind. Some find it effective to use music to accompany a reading or a spoken prayer. They also report that this practice offers a useful opportunity for clergy and musicians to plan together.

Some, however, would strongly disagree about mixing music and words.

> 'I sometimes wonder at people who talk over the music. It's a bit like introducing folk to a work of art while you block the view by standing in front of it.'
>
> 'I attended a Jewish service in Jerusalem and discovered at various stages there was a kind of interlude where the worship leaders were doing their bit at the front, the musicians were playing quietly in the background, and the congregation were moving about and engaging in conversation. And it worked! The suggestion being that there is a place for listening to music and a time for it to be in the background . . . a time for conversation and a time for quiet reverence.'

Words can also be sung, and often are. If the words have real significance, it is important that they can be heard and understood, and that is not always the case when a text is sung.

> 'Words to anthems are now included in the Order of Service, and that has been appreciated by members of the congregation who were struggling to hear the words.'

Setting the mood before the commencement of a service is important.

> 'I try to play several pieces of music in preparation for the service, gradually bringing the mood down and trying to prepare the congregation.'
>
> 'I think that a couple of voluntaries before the service can be really effective.'
>
> 'I try to play at least one hymn prelude before the service, perhaps based on one of the hymns we are about to sing or one related to the season of the year.'
>
> 'Nobody listens to what I play before the service. They all natter their heads off.'

These views suggest that some musicians give considerable time and preparation to what they play before the service but that the congregation do not always listen. Perhaps the congregation in your church do listen and therefore the music has an opportunity to affect them. And if they don't listen, are you clear in your own mind about what you are trying to achieve in that time before the commencement of the formal time of worship? Maybe you could share your thoughts with the congregation as part of an exercise to discover how you could achieve the aim more effectively.

In some churches the clergy and choir, if there is one, arrive in church early. That acts as a signal for the congregation to rise and then subside to listen to the music, giving it a chance to speak.

Some churches find it effective to use a 'gathering hymn' to promote a mood of coming together in worship.

Music is born out of silence, in so far as we can ever experience silence. Musicians understand the value of silence: that concentrated moment before the music begins, that magic moment after the last notes have melted away, those powerful silences punctuating powerful chords. Without the silences the chords would be nothing. One organist told us he hesitates to 'fill' the gaps in services as sometimes silence can be more eloquent. Equally, we may sometimes have been inclined to look in the 'driving mirror' to check whether the officiating priest/minister has gone home, when a sudden unexplained silence has replaced the announcement of a hymn.

> 'I'm currently encouraging our worship leaders to pause, say after a reading or prayer, before announcing a hymn, as these spaces are terribly important and prevent the service feeling rushed. I also like services with no announcements, allowing the organist to determine the correct length of silences – they're often in a better place to judge.'

Questions for discussion

- Why do some clergy use too many words?
- Why do some musicians use too many notes?
- How can silence be effective in worship?
- How is it effective in your worship?
- Are there moments in your worship when music could be juxtaposed with silence?
- How can you be daring enough to use music to find the silences?

If it is part of the organist's job to create music when otherwise there might be a quiet moment, perhaps we need to consider the difference between a quiet moment and a moment when nothing seems to be happening.

Experiences

Worship is not only a response to God but also an experience of God. The word 'experience' is one that needs some exploration. A friend had a conversation with a minister in which they hit on the notion of a 'musical experience'. The conversation was going well until the friend made the mistake of moving it towards the differences and similarities between a musical experience and a religious experience. Yet those differences are worth exploring.

You will more than likely have listened to a musical performance and felt elated as a result. Perhaps, as a result of another performance, you have found yourself transported into a world of calm and peace. In the process you will have become one with the performing musicians, and arguably with the composer whose music they were re-creating. You have shared a musical experience. That musical experience is one type of aesthetic experience. The high drama of some forms of worship could be another example.

Distinguishing a musical experience and an experience of God raises huge philosophical issues. However, all good things come from God, and the distinctions may not be as important as our response. As A. E. Taylor once wrote, 'If William Shakespeare walked into a room we would stand, if Jesus Christ walked into the room we would kneel.'[2] Our task, as clergy and musicians, is to work and plan together to invite the right response to our experiences in worship.

Questions for discussion

- What is a 'musical experience'?
- How can it be of value in worship?
- Why would you value aesthetic experiences in your worship?
- How can you ensure that music in your church helps to create such an experience?

Many churches do not find it easy to recruit musicians. Sometimes that difficulty leads to 'getting by' with musicians who, on their own admission, struggle with technical difficulties. The resulting fragility in the quality of the performance can make the sharing of a musical experience virtually impossible. Too many wrong notes, hesitations and slack rhythm can easily destroy any aesthetic quality. We may well admire those who struggle to play or sing while battling with technical difficulties, determined not to give up, but at the same time the outcomes of their endeavours may not result in music that can 'take us to God.' In some services that will be more of a problem than in others, and the process may be highly beneficial to the embryonic musician, enabling them to grow in confidence. Every church surely has a responsibility to make help available to a musician who is giving their time and energy to the service of that church.

Why sing?

One of the roles of music in worship would seem to be related to singing, if we can believe the evidence of our ears! Yet sometimes we have wondered whether setting words to music is always beneficial to the words. We confess to having launched with great enthusiasm into a favourite tune, only to realise after the event that such was our involvement that the words passed us by completely. We also confess that, in non-conformist services where ministers often read part of the hymn prior to singing it, we have sometimes been suddenly struck by the meaning of the words when they are read rather than sung.

Can setting poetry to music enhance the message of the words? Can it also detract from the message of the words?

---

2. A.E. Taylor, 'The Argument from Religious Experience' in John Hick (ed.), *The Existence of God* (USA: Macmillan, 1964), p.159.

> 'I transpose most congregational hymns down. I believe that the average range of an untrained singer is probably around A to A and I try to pitch the tunes so that singer can sing.'
>
> 'If you transpose the music down, those who sing in their boots, an octave too low, will not love you.'
>
> 'I jolly well make my congregation work. They need to get their lungs going and produce some breath support. I'm not in the business of making it easier for them.'
>
> 'Transposing it down – isn't that a bit like "dumbing it down"?'
>
> 'The vicar tried to get the congregation to sit closer together in the centre section. They didn't take too easily to that idea but I don't see how they can sing when few of them stand within ten feet of the next person. Who would arrange a group of singers like that?'

We are rarely members of the congregation, but when we have been, we have sometimes found singing to be an uncomfortable experience. Sometimes that has resulted from feeling that we were performing a solo, perhaps the result of choosing to sit too far away from other members of the congregation. In some churches the congregation are actively encouraged to sit together as a group in order to address this problem.

> 'I was heavily criticised at college during a sermon class because I created worship "in the round" in the anti-chapel. One tutor commented that he hadn't liked it because he'd had to "look at others throughout".'

Sometimes our discomfort has been because the range of notes was too high. There is a working range of notes that can be sung by most of the population. We may deprecate it, but that range is quite limited and is also slowly descending. This descent in range may be the outcome of physiological changes that have resulted from a general increased quality of life in our society over the past few hundred years. It may be further exacerbated by the increased average age of congregations, as the voice has a tendency to drop in pitch with age.

It is possible to transpose music for congregational singing. Some may not consider such a practice to be desirable. Certainly, if you are working with a choir, altos and basses will not enjoy grovelling in the depths. You may also feel that you are pandering to so-called 'lazy singers', and the musician quoted above who is determined to make her congregation 'work' would most certainly agree with that view.

Oddly, those who 'sing in their boots' will not thank you either, as their 'boots' will not reach low enough to match your transposed pitch.

> 'At a wedding that involved the managers of a local public house, their regulars sat at the back and sang "All Things Bright and Beautiful" raucously, as if they were at a football ground. I loved their rendition as it was full of passion – but the organist played through gritted teeth!'

We may have something to learn from corporate singing in other activities. Football fans, who probably would not sing anywhere else, sing at matches. They do so in a tightly packed group and relate very closely to that group.

> 'A freezing Saturday in February. A packed football ground in England. The match is tense. The ref gives a free kick. The crowd stamps and jeers and shouts, a song swells and stirs from the stands ... The tune is a hymn. The words are not.'[3]

Singing can bring people together and can engender a sense of fellowship and community. That sense of fellowship and community is surely just as relevant and important in worship as it is in a football stadium.

Enabling the worshippers to feel part of a community can transform worship. It can also attract more participants.

Questions for discussion

- How can you encourage worshippers to feel part of a fellowship?
- How can you try to make the fellowship, found in musical performance in your church, more effective?

The benefits of singing

Putting aside some of the positive outcomes that might accrue from a closer fellowship, we could consider singing as an activity in its own right. If we examine some of the possible physical benefits, we find that singing can:

- help to exercise our lungs;
- help to tone up our intercostal muscles and our diaphragm;
- help to improve our sleep;
- benefit our heart and circulation by improving our aerobic capacity;

---

3. Andrew Gant, *O Sing unto the Lord*, p.vii.

- help to decrease muscle tension;
- help to tone our facial muscles;
- help our posture;
- help us to stay mentally alert;
- help to keep the sinuses and respiratory tubes open;
- even assist in the release of pain-relieving endorphins;
- boost our immune system.

It might be worthwhile to share the news of these benefits with our worshipping community.

If we examine some of the possible emotional benefits of singing, we find that it can:

- increase self-esteem and confidence;
- increase feelings of well-being;
- enhance mood;
- be useful as a stress reducer;
- help reduce anger, depression and anxiety;
- be uplifting spiritually;
- increase positive feelings;
- encourage creativity;
- be energising;
- promote bonding;
- increase understanding and empathy between cultures.

You might well come to the conclusion that some, if not all, of these benefits are fairly fundamental to worship.

> 'It is also beneficial in the period after worship, as many people comment that they find themselves singing a hymn in the hours after worship.'

TWO

Working together

> 'There is something in the make-up of clergy and organists which on occasion impels them to behave both irresponsibly and irrationally. Obvious to all are the repercussions of two apparently responsible adults, both in prominent parochial positions, being unable to see eye to eye. Much harm can be done to the cause of the Church by the inevitable tongue wagging which accompanies such incidents.'[4]

> 'When it comes to music it is rather like flower arrangements – I don't want anything to do with that.'

Many musicians would be quite happy with that arrangement. So might many flower arrangers. P. D. James wrote:

> 'There were the seemingly inevitable disputes at Easter-time and Harvest Festival about who should and should not decorate the altar and pulpit, and my mother voiced her dissatisfaction at always being given one of the darkest windows. There were the usual arguments between the organist and the vicar about the hymns and the music.'[5]

Are such disputes inevitable? Is it not the case that the expertise and wisdom of both could, in combination, make for more memorable and effective services?

It comes with a history

Disputes between clergy and musicians are not new. Those familiar with the diaries of Parson Woodforde will remember that in 1769 he recorded that he had ordered the choir of his Somerset parish to say rather than sing the responses. Sadly, his order was not obeyed, and the choir duly sang the first response. The parson was therefore moved to remonstrate with them from his stall. Such a public admonishment did not please the members of the choir, who consequently absented themselves from the church altogether.

J. S. Bach's career was bedevilled by disputes. In 1706 he was castigated by his employers for 'having hitherto made many curious variations to the chorale, and mingled many strange tones in it'.[6] He

4. Lionel Dakers, *Church Music at the Crossroads* (London: Marshall, Morgan and Scott, 1970), p.86.
5. P.D. James, *Time to be in Earnest: A Fragment of Autobiography* (London: Faber & Faber, 1999), p.281.
6. Jacques Attali (translated by Brian Massumi), *Noise: Political Economy of Music (Theory & History of Literature)*, (University of Minnesota Press, June 1985), p.18.

complained later that 'the authorities are hard to please and care little for music'.[7]

In 2013 Christian Research, a polling and research group, asked its 2000-strong 'Resonate' panel of churchgoers for their views on church music and organists. Of those who responded, half said they had noticed an organist slip unexpected tunes into services. An organist in Scotland who had fallen out with some of the elders in the Kirk inserted a thinly disguised rendition of 'Send in the clowns' as they processed in for a Sunday service. Elsewhere, a vicar sacked an organist after he played 'Roll out the Barrel' at the funeral of a man known to have been fond of a drink. Members of another congregation found themselves passing around the collection plate to the strains of 'Money, money, money' by Abba. One organist who responded confessed to playing hits by Oasis, Billy Bragg and even Kylie Minogue in services, but added, 'Nobody notices – I do it all the time.'

> 'One of my services had focused on the sins of humankind, with the organist offering an impromptu rendition of "Ain't misbehavin'" during the taking up of the offertory.'

Some of these tales may be apocryphal; others the mischievous organist's equivalent of the medieval builder who carved high in the church roof a boss of a woman exposing her bottom to the clergy below. Yet the well-known joke, 'What's the difference between an organist and a terrorist? You can negotiate with a terrorist', suggests something far more inflammatory and widely acknowledged.

Church organists are often distanced physically from the minister and congregation, and this can lead to a sense of alienation. There is also the view that each has a mutually exclusive area of expertise.

The musical view

> 'You know you have real trouble when the clergy think they know about music.'
>
> 'May the Lord save me from a parson who "knows about music".'
>
> 'I wouldn't dream of telling him what to say in his sermons.'
>
> 'I find it difficult to reconcile the needs of the choral tradition with what the minister regards as the needs of the community, but not many of them come to church in any case.'

---

7. Joe Staines, *The Rough Guide to Classical Music*, p.18.

Sometimes this comes about as a result of the organist seeing shortcomings in the musical ability of the minister.

> 'The trouble is that she thinks that she can sing.'
>
> 'Is it unrealistic to expect to receive the hymns and details for the service before I arrive at church?'
>
> 'A favourite trick is changing the order of the hymns and expecting me to be on the right page.'

Some organists will have experienced a member of the clergy who believes they can sing or play the piano or organ and whose efforts leave something to be desired. Some will have had to face comments from the congregation about why we 'let him sing those solos', and perhaps have had to admit that we don't 'let him' but that he rather 'lets himself'.

Our business is the duty and joy of worship, and both minister and musician need to recognise that collaboration is required. A good piece of music and a good sermon don't necessarily combine to make good worship. The music must support, balance or contrast with the tone of the sermon, and both must be meaningful to the congregation. As we mentioned earlier, no film is produced without careful and painstaking cooperation between the composer of the score and the director in deciding where music should be used, what style is appropriate and what effect is desired. The expertise of clergy and organist must be brought together.

There is no mystery about collaboration. It requires time to meet, prepare and express appreciation. It requires honesty in expressing differences and airing grievances, and in recognising ability and limitations. Yet our research shows that often these basic elements are absent.

> 'It would be nice if the priest just gave a hint that he appreciated the music from time to time.'
>
> 'The first thing I try to do is express my heartfelt thanks to the organist and choir prior to meeting the congregation at the door. It is my way of acknowledging the importance of others in the provision of worship and ought to be impressed on all who lead worship.'

Most clergy find time to talk to those leading intercessions about the theme of their sermon and about those for whom it would be appropriate to pray. Musicians need to have the same sort of conversation. Musicians will need to have time to check the appropriate nature of the set tunes for hymns and decide whether any descants or alternative harmonisations are appropriate. They will want to decide whether any tunes need to be transposed. They will want to rehearse any unfamiliar points themselves and with the choir or music group. Some musicians will need to reassure themselves that they can play the notes. If the quality of the music in the service is to be as high as possible, the choir or music group must have sufficient time for thorough rehearsal, and it is quite unacceptable to expect otherwise.

Furthermore, there will occasionally be unforeseen circumstances that can result in last-minute adjustments being necessary on the day.

From time to time relations reach a point of no return.

> 'He won't listen to me and I've had enough.'
>
> 'I played over the hymn and his booming voice said, "We are not going to use that tune." I just said, "Oh yes we are," and carried on with it.'
>
> 'I had previously requested that the Lord's Prayer be sung in the service and was assured that this would not be a problem. When it came to that point the organ remained silent but the organist's voice issued forth, "Our Father . . ." The congregation followed like lambs.'
>
> 'Music at my church is really under threat.'

How tragic and immature when ultimatums are issued from either side.

> 'We had a minister who insisted that the voluntaries were no longer than one and a half minutes.'

How much better to air any differences at an earlier date, clear the air and settle upon a working relationship that produces meaningful worship. It is often too late once crisis point is reached and such unseemly interactions as those cited above have been played out in the public arena.

While musicians sometimes consider that the clergy take too much interest in the music, we have also been offered comments from musicians who feel that in their church the clergy do not take any interest in the music.

> 'She said, "I don't know the first thing about music so just get on with it your way."'
>
> 'After the service there is a prayer in the vestry. Would it hurt just to say a few words of thanks to the choir at that point?'

Yet there are many churches in which clergy and musicians have a happy working relationship where each respect and admire the other.

> 'Our minister is the best ever. We have frequent meetings and talk about what is coming up and what she would like the outcomes to be and how we might achieve those outcomes.'

> 'There always seems to be something in each service that he really enjoyed or found moving, and he always tells me.'

The clerical view

The complaints of lack of musical ability and sensitivity levelled against the clergy are also reflected in comments offered by members of the clergy.

> 'She plays hymns so slowly.'

> 'He seems to play the music as fast as possible. I cannot keep up.'

> 'I don't know how you are supposed to take a breath at that speed.'

> 'She gives no lead to the congregation.'

> 'He plays over a hymn and I am still left wondering what the tune is.'

A variant of this would seem to be the failure of the musician to appreciate what musical skills might be expected from the clergy.

> 'He knows I'm not a great singer but he keeps coming out with new things for me to sing in the service, all without any preparation.'

And that magic word 'preparation' is an important element. Perhaps the musical contribution could be made easier with some preparation, help and support from the professional.

In the same way that the clergy have been criticised for lack of preparation and notice of intent, sadly musicians fall into the same trap.

> 'The church secretary sends out the details for next Sunday each Tuesday and then the organist wants to alter it at 10.25 on Sunday morning.'

Appreciating the efforts of the other and making sure that the appreciation is voiced is key. A realistic view of the ability of the other is also important and would prevent situations where a priest or minister with limited musical ability is forced to contemplate an embarrassing contribution to worship foisted on them by their organist. It would also prevent the embarrassment of a reluctant organist, who is doing their best to help, being faced with a request for music that is much too difficult.

Perhaps both musicians and clergy need to have a realistic view of their own musical talents. Is it better to play a voluntary within your technical range or to struggle through endless semiquavers inflicting far too many wrong ones, delivered with the assistance of full organ, on the unfortunate listeners? Is it likely to foster good working relationships if you argue with your fully qualified organist, who has known the congregation for twice as long as you, over the most appropriate tune for a hymn?

> 'I had training in voice production, but no instructions on church music and relationship with organist and choirs. This is a gap that needs filling.'

A brighter view

Our research also revealed good practice. We recently saw this email from a minister to the organist – one who operates on a rota.

> 'I see that you are down to play for our Remembrance Sunday morning service in three weeks' time. I am beginning to plan that as I will be away next week for half term.
>
> 'If you have any thoughts at this stage about appropriate music I would greatly appreciate them. Currently I am working on the possibility of having a prelude in place of songs of gathering, and a piece of music after maybe a poem or meditation (yet to be determined) that offers space for congregational reflection. Naturally there will be an organ postlude.
>
> 'When I have readings/hymns etc. in draft form I will send them through again for your comments.'

Well, there is an example to follow. The organist's skills are clearly appreciated, and advice was sought at an early stage in preparation for what was to be a special service. The email speaks volumes for the acknowledgement of teamwork, and the minister's understanding of what the organist can offer to the process. The minister is giving thought to how the service should begin and how the congregation can best be drawn together in fellowship. He requests a prelude from the organist, and that will provide a challenge if the task is to be accomplished effectively. He further plans for a musical offering in order to allow time for contemplation on a poem or meditation – another challenge for the organist.

The reply from the organist thanked the minister for inviting input and offered several suggestions. The organist lives about 40 minutes' drive from the church. He offered the minister a meeting by phone or Skype, during which he might play over some extracts from pieces of music in order that the minister and musician might choose items together.

Understanding the other view

Meetings between clergy and organists are seemingly fairly rare in many places. They are also not always productive. We recently witnessed a meeting with a new minister during which the organist pointed out, with great courtesy, that the congregation would not know either of the set tunes to a particular hymn and that there were very few, if any, alternatives. With some trepidation the organist played over a tune that he had taken time to compose during the week. It was deliberately designed to be reasonably easy for the congregation. The minister decided to use one of the set tunes. On any level that might appear to be a strange decision.

Being open to the views of the other party might be a key. Trying to understand why the other party has a particular opinion could be another. Making opinions transparent could help understanding.

A decision to speak the three collects in a Choral Evensong might be understood from the point of view of involving the congregation, especially if the third collect were to be said together by all those present. It might also be understood from the point of view of a priest who cannot intone in tune, although there is no reason why a member of the choir should not act as cantor. At the same time, saying the collects would preclude the choir from singing their well-rehearsed 'amen' at the end of each prayer, particularly the florid 'amen' after the third collect. The question then to be asked might relate to the perceived and agreed priorities for a very choir-based service such as Choral Evensong.

Integrated working

Some of the most fruitful instances of working together come from worship teams. There are many examples in which members of a worship team meet regularly. The team comprises clergy, lay ministers, musicians and others involved in planning the services and their content. Discussion leads to decisions about the nature of the worship and the content for the coming months. If the direction of the services is going to be guided by the lectionary, then there will be discussion about what emphasis will emerge to give focus and direction to each service. This will present inspiration for sermons, prayers and music.

A very worthwhile extension of this principle has emerged in some churches in which the worship team has developed into a ministry team. This team will comprise all those outlined above but will also include representatives of those involved in the greater ministry of that particular church, including the pastoral team. So those who visit the sick, operate chaplaincies and operate outreach into the community in any way will be represented along with those responsible for rotas of preachers and musicians. The team can discuss the current situation and challenges facing the church fellowship in the most inclusive terms. Special cases and needs within the congregation or the community at large are frequently part of the discussion, and music will be one item on the agenda. The team will decide at times that a break from the lectionary is needed in order to visit a particular concern or reason for celebration within the church or the community. A series of services with a special focus might well emerge.

> 'In preparation for a particular initiative to reach out into the community we abandoned the lectionary for a period of weeks and each service was planned to focus on a particular point or set of points which non-Christians might be expected to raise.'

One musical director working with such a system related the normal practice:

> 'The week before the service I will already have an outline of the service and Bible readings. I have that from being part of the ministry team. As an example I already know that in Lent next year we shall be concentrating on "giving". At that point I receive an outline of the sermon. In some cases that could be a series of bullet points. Those can be very useful. In other cases, particularly with some visiting preachers, the outline could be as brief as "The Good Shepherd", and not so useful. From there, choosing the music is down to me. I will prepare hymns and other music to complement the chosen elements of the service. Some preachers will make a request, when they send the sermon outline, for a particular hymn or piece of music and I will always do my best to include it if possible.'

Not only does such a ministry team have the opportunity to plan for direction and progression in the flow of services, but they also have the opportunity to relate different services to different potential groups of worshippers and different groups within the wider community. So the nature of a family service or a Choral Evensong can be a shared responsibility, and at whom that service is aimed will also be clear.

Such groups still face the problems experienced in other working practices. However, they will have time to resolve those problems, and from discussions between several parties the prospect of far more significant and stimulating worship will emerge.

The discussions will not be restricted to the priest or minister and the musical director. With others involved, the very sad and destructive confrontations witnessed too often between clergy and musicians might be more easily avoided.

Church music, like all elements of church practice, arises from communities. The Gospels and Epistles reflect the concerns of the church communities with which the early evangelists and apostles were associated. As we compare a Gothic Revivalist church by Pugin or Liverpool's Metropolitan Cathedral, styles of church architecture evolve from theology and practice. Church music is no different. From plainsong to Taizé chants, from Wesley hymns to Darlene Zschech songs, church music arises from church communities of all kinds. If the music of our churches is to be vibrant and attractive, serving the ministry of worship and evangelism, it too must arise from our church communities. That can only come from the community coming together and working collaboratively, giving time to understand its theology and practice, the capability of its members and the music that expresses both heartfelt joy and wonder.

> 'At one of my churches, I am encouraging the creation of a Worship Planning Group, to which all worship leaders and those wanting to be more involved would be invited. The idea would be to share ideas in the preparation of worship, as well as to reflect on previous worship experiences.'

Questions for discussion

- What benefit might there be if music in your church were to be planned over a period of time so that themes can be explored in depth?
- What benefit might there be if a wider team than clergy and musicians were involved?
- Is the musician always given sufficient time to prepare music to a high standard?
- Is the musician always given sufficient information about the content of the service in order to enable choice of music to be made in support of that content?
- Does planning for a service always need to start with the clergy?
- As a musician, do you give the priest or minister sufficient notification of musical decisions?
- What benefit might there be in musicians sharing explanations for musical decisions?
- What practices could clergy and musicians introduce in order to establish a transparent framework of mutual respect?

THREE

Hymns

> 'Our selection of hymns that the congregation know is limited and must seem very antique to younger people.'
>
> 'The congregation tends to look backwards rather than forwards.'
>
> 'The worst thing is playing for weddings and funerals. The vicar lets them choose hymns and then nobody knows them – even "All Things Bright and Beautiful", which is the favourite.'

A culture of hymns

It is claimed that the world's longest-running religious television show is the BBC's *Songs of Praise*, a programme devoted to hymn-singing and attracting up to two million viewers each week. The 50-plus years since its first programme in October 1961 have seen a huge change in the nation's hymn-singing. At its height, audience figures reached more than eight million, and the programme was broadcast from one location with the congregation singing a variety of hymns. At the end of 2014, Aaqil Ahmed, the BBC's head of religion, declared the average age of its audience to be in their mid-seventies. In an attempt to attract a new audience, including British immigrants, and to reflect the changing nature of Christian music, the programme began to be broadcast from multiple locations and churches of different denominations.

The reality of the changing nature of hymn-singing in our churches is evident at funerals. Funerals requiring an organ are mostly attended by members of a generation which have at least a nodding acquaintance with the hymn repertoire. They were encouraged to sing, and may indeed have sung hymns in assemblies at school even if their attendance at church was limited. Few are the schools making any attempt to keep alive a culture of hymns in the twenty-first century. And so the bereaved relatives will choose some hymns for the service, and then they will not sing them. It is a hard conclusion to reach, but would it be better not to offer them the option in the first place?

We might wonder why they choose the hymns that appear on the smartly printed service sheets. Was 'All Things Bright and Beautiful' really that popular, or is it the only title that they recognise? Are there hymns that are still part of our culture today, and will there be any in ten years' time?

Most new movements or new ways of looking at worship have stimulated new music, and the contemporary worship movement is no exception. Much of what is being created has greater links to the world of pop music and pop culture. Superficially, many modern songs might be regarded as more 'of the people', and probably they are in a style more widely recognised and appreciated. Even so, it is increasingly difficult for newly created religious work, in any style, to become part of the culture of a nation.

Words in hymns

> 'The vicar chooses hymns and I don't understand half the words.'
>
> 'I would like to use hymns with words that might mean something to the average member of the congregation but the vicar blocks their use because he says nobody will know them.'

The musician who tells us he does not understand the meaning of 'half the words' is not alone. It was ever so. We report a childhood conviction that 'He who would valiant be' must be a New Zealand hymn because 'His strength the more is'. We are also reminded of the moment of light when a scientific colleague explained the 'famous stone' of George Herbert's 'Teach me, my God and King, in all things thee to see.'[8]

Some members of the congregation might struggle with theological references in some hymns. They might struggle with the language used, yet many of the hymns have remained popular owing to their coupling with a favourite tune. We could just give up and stop using hymns where language or reference is obscure. We could also take the obscurity as a challenge and find ways to enable understanding.

Questions for discussion

- If you examine the hymns that were sung in your church last Sunday, what difficulties might some of the words create for some members of the congregation?
- What could you do about that?
- Some churches have found that a series of articles in their magazine, a series of sermons highlighting particular hymns, a series of short printed monthly notes, or a series of notes online have been helpful. But which, if any, of those might work to the benefit of your congregation?

---

8. The line reads, 'This is the famous stone that turneth all to gold.' It is a reference to the Philosopher's Stone, a legendary entity and subject of the quest undertaken by many alchemists. It was said to be capable of turning base metals such as lead into gold.

Can the congregation have a view?

> 'I believe I have a pretty fair idea of what they thought about the hymns and the tunes. They don't mind telling me on their way out!'

In some churches the congregation's views on hymns are happily sought. Those who have tried such a survey relate that the take-up is small and that views tend to be expressed by a few members of the congregation only. Mostly, a simple box into which ideas can be posted seems to be used. Perhaps there could be benefit in setting up an online forum: it might attract comments from a different age range. Surprisingly few churches use the internet in more than the most basic way. You may need to safeguard the professional standing of the organist and the clergy from abuse.

One church recently opened up a competition to the congregation, inviting them to write the words for a hymn in 2015. The results were not numerically huge but they were well worth singing.

Selecting hymns

In some places, choosing hymns is part of the role of the organist; in others it falls to the clergy. In other churches the clergy choose the hymns and the organist tries to influence the choice of tunes. In some churches there will be a group set up for the purpose of planning all aspects of the services, including the hymns. We might note that the job of choosing the hymns is often one that relies on the tradition of the particular church. New clergy have been known to compare the discovery of 'who' and 'why' with attempting to cross a minefield blindfolded.

Having decided who might choose the hymns, how they choose them is the next point for consideration.

> 'In the back of my hymn book I have a short list of my favourite hymns and, if the preacher does not send through their choices before choir practice, I choose some from my list and it is done.'

> 'The hymns are chosen by a person who does not have a strong feel for what might suit a particular service.'

> 'I use the lectionary to gain inspiration for which hymns might add another level of meaning to the service.'

> 'I have a list of hymns that they like, know and can sing, and I choose them from that.'

> 'In the index section of the hymn book is a section based on topics, and I try to find a fit with the theme for the day.'

> 'I love the cycle of the church year and I love the way hymns reflect that cycle.'
>
> 'It depends on what sort of service it is – families – older folk – children.'
>
> 'I'll know, well in advance, what the intention of the service is and can select hymns to reinforce that.'
>
> 'I believe that you must start with the people you expect to be in church – their lives, joys and sorrows. That chooses the hymns for you.'

The last quotation certainly marks a radical approach, and yet it is an approach that is likely to make an impact and a connection with the lives of the worshippers.

When you know that the church will be full, do you choose hymns that visitors might recognise and enjoy?

> 'I've given up going at Christmas. You can't even join in and have a good sing. The hymns are just ridiculous. I don't know any of them – not a single carol.'

Sometimes the tune set in the book will be one that the congregation will not know. You may well feel that they should know it and set about educating them. Alternatively, you might decide to choose another tune that will fit. The first step is probably to consult the metrical index in the book. In theory, if the metre is the same the tune should fit, but it is not that easy. You will need to consider the feel and mood of the new tune. You may need to consider the words at points where the new tune rises to a climax. Does that chime with a parallel moment in the words?

A *Songs of Praise* event

A service based on hymns is a popular event in some churches. Whether the priest or minister will be able to resist the temptation to preach a sermon is one consideration. Here are some more.

Questions for discussion

- What might be the benefits from holding a *Songs of Praise* type service based on hymns?
- How could you design the service in order to offer opportunities for:
  - introducing a new hymn or new tune?
  - the congregation and choir to choose some of the hymns?
  - those choosing hymns to say a little about why they made those choices?

Introducing new repertoire

> 'We have a problem introducing new hymns.'
>
> 'Our congregation are very reluctant to learn new hymns.'
>
> 'The vicar expects me to have a hymn practice before the service starts.'
>
> 'When necessary we have a short rehearsal with the congregation prior to the service.'
>
> 'I make sure that I play the tune of the new hymn as a "fill" at various points in the service before we sing it.'
>
> 'The band will play a new song as the "voluntary" before the service, or if it is reflective then we might well sing it during communion.'
>
> 'There is a real danger that I'll fall back on my favourites so I keep a spreadsheet that shows the regularity in use of any hymn. It is also useful for making a performing rights return.'

Many find learning a new tune difficult. If someone played you an unknown hymn tune once, would you be able to sing it? Those who mock the simplicity of repetitive tasks in lower grades of music examinations should also note the regularity with which some of the candidates fail to repeat even a simple, short phrase. They are taking music lessons.

Inviting the congregation to sing through a new tune several times before the service begins pays dividends. Some churches even integrate the rehearsal into the service so that the tune is fresh in the mind. There are churches that have a policy to sing the same new hymn twice in the service; others sing the same new hymn for weeks in a row. Whichever practice you adopt, it could be beneficial to explain to the congregation what you intend and why. It might be illuminating to ask the views of the congregation. How do they think they could learn new tunes?

Even if you prefer not to go down the 'rehearsal' route, you can still offer support to the congregation in unfamiliar tunes. 'Soloing' the melody can be effective, bearing in mind that it's always easier to tune in to the melody if it is played in a different octave from the singers. So the melody could be played an octave higher or lower on a different manual from the harmony. That is not the easiest task and may call for some extra preparation. Some hymns lend themselves to being played with sparse harmony, thus making the melody more obvious to the congregation. A choir singing in unison can also help to lead the congregation in an unfamiliar repertoire.

The introduction of new hymns offers a good opportunity for discussion between the clergy and the musicians. Representatives of the congregation could also be included.

Hymns with repetitive words

> 'I cannot see the point of repeating four lines over and over. It's even worse when it is one line.'
>
> 'It allows the lyrics to soak in. In a normal hymn there's lots of content, but repetition allows focus on individual words almost in a meditative way.'
>
> 'In the mechanics of putting a service together we plan perhaps to drop down to an instrumental or at least to vary the instrumentation when the words are repetitive.'
>
> 'As you read the words over and over you have time to contemplate each phrase and the significance of the words.'
>
> 'I think there is a danger that it can just become repetitive and the meaning is lost.'

This issue has huge hackle-raising potential. Perhaps the key is to ask what purpose the repetitions serve and how they can be most effective.

Is the task of playing hymns in a service as simple as it might seem?

> 'The band take the preparation of the hymns very seriously, so that we can provide a varied accompaniment in different verses and give added significance to the lyrics.'

Fashions in playing for services come and go. Those who are 'dedicated followers of fashion' will be well provided for, with ready-made answers. Others may wish to ask some questions about playing for hymns. For some musicians, playing the notes will be challenge enough. Others may wish to contemplate a more vibrant and varied style of accompaniment.

Questions for discussion

Here are some thinking and discussion points for musicians. Clergy may well also have some ideas.

- Why do you always play hymns in the set key?
- Why do you play all hymns at the same speed?
- Might it be effective to vary the tempo within some hymns? Why?
- What are the advantages/disadvantages of using the same accompaniment for every verse?

- What are the advantages/disadvantages in maintaining the same length of gap between verses in every hymn?
- How can you help to bring a hymn alive?
- How can you use changes in registration to add interest to hymns?
- How can you 'play the words' as well as the music?
- How can you use different registers of the organ to add effect to the organ accompaniment?

Playing over

The play-over is the first clue offered to the congregation about what tune is being used, and the tempo at which it is intended that the hymn should be sung. There is little point therefore in playing over at a different tempo from that which you intend to use for the hymn.

The play-over is often treated in the same way, with little regard for the nature of the hymn or its position in the service.

> 'I always play the first two lines of the hymn on the swell and then move to the great for the first verse.'
>
> 'I think it is good practice to play the introduction on the same registration that I intend to use for the first verse.'

Depending on when you had organ lessons and who taught you, you might recognise one of the two suggestions above. Hymns have their own character, so we should like to enter a plea for consideration about how you introduce a hymn. There is no point in playing the introduction so quietly that it is difficult to hear, but for some hymns a single melody line played on a flute stop can be very effective. For another hymn an introduction on a trumpet stop might be more in keeping. For another hymn an introduction played on full swell could set the appropriate mood. And 'appropriate mood' is the challenging aim. We offered above the notion of introducing the tune and the tempo, but introducing the mood is also important.

Some hymns are very effectively introduced with full harmony. For others, a single line of melody will be more effective.

> 'Oh yes – our organist likes his one-finger exercises.'

For some hymns, the single-line melody played in octaves will provide an invigorating introduction. For others, it is effective to begin the play-over with the melody, shortly adding in an alto part and then perhaps adding the tenor and bass parts.

Where you stop the play-over is also a point for consideration. It pays to consider the relationship between the stopping point and the first chords of the hymn. Those organists who always play over the first two lines may not always produce the most musical of effects.

Some hymns are so familiar that playing over the last two lines is much more effective in providing a link back to the opening. The congregation, hearing the end of the hymn, are subconsciously prepared to sing the opening of the hymn.

Working with a choir

> 'I try to make sure that there is always one hymn with a descant or other special treatment for at least one verse in every service.'
>
> 'What they really hate is when the visiting preacher chooses a whole load of unison hymns.'

If you are lucky enough to have a choir to work with, you will be conscious of the need to maintain a level of challenge for them. Tension between clergy and musicians can often be sparked by disagreements concerning the role of the choir in a service. If the choir is not allowed to use its musical talents, members will soon lose interest.

Questions for discussion

- What hymns does your choir enjoy singing?
- How could you build challenge for the choir into the performance of hymns?
- What might be the advantages/disadvantages in arranging for the choir to:
  - sing special verses in some hymns?
  - sing descants in some verses?
  - sing descants in most hymns?
- What is the value of unison verses within a hymn?
- Do you try to choose hymns to reflect a mix of unison and part singing?
- When could the use of a solo verse be effective?

Leading the singing

> 'The priest is keen that I should play loudly in order to give what he calls a "strong lead" to the congregation.'
>
> 'I like to hear the congregation singing and so I vary the accompaniment to suit their need for support.'

> 'I particularly value an organist who has a good feel for the words and is able to convey appropriate moods in the way they accompany the hymn, e.g. holding the congregation back in quiet phrases and encouraging the congregation to "let rip" through crescendos.'

For the congregation, a hymn is important as it is an opportunity to take an active role in the service. A part of the musician's task is to lead and support the singing; congregations left without support will soon lose confidence. The level of 'leading' and 'supporting' will vary from hymn to hymn and even from verse to verse. It will also vary from congregation to congregation. In a well-known hymn, the level of support might be quite different from that in a less familiar tune. If the congregation is singing well it may be more effective, if your skills allow, to lighten the accompaniment and add more variety to it at the same time. A verse without pedals, a verse with lighter chordal treatment, particularly in unison hymns, a verse in which the choir leads can all add life and variety to the accompaniment. All those decisions need to be made within an understanding of the words of the hymn.

Part of your planning for the service will be to decide where you can allow the congregation the thrill of hearing the full organ or the band really 'going to town'. Finding the high spot in the service can help to underline the structure. Deciding how the other hymns fit into that structure will also add significance.

> 'Can we not think a little outside the box for our musical resources? I've seen several parishes where a group from the congregation volunteer to turn up to weddings and funerals to form a core of worshippers, injected into the congregation, to sing the hymns and pray the prayers.'

Well, there's a revolutionary idea.

The last resort or a golden opportunity?

> 'We have no organist so we sing hymns from a CD.'
>
> 'CDs are very important to us.'
>
> 'Making do with a CD is a very poor substitute.'

In churches where no organist can be found, a system of pre-recorded music is sometimes seen as the last resort for leading the singing. At the most basic this can mean using CDs. At a more advanced level there are packages available that offer greater flexibility. Many offer thousands of hymns in various forms together with organ voluntaries and even service settings. Costs can be as low as less than 25p for a hymn, and selections are available for weddings, funerals, junior church, Christmas, Lent, Easter, Remembrance (including the bugle calls) and much more. In one installation the speakers were hidden in the apse and the resulting sound made for an unforgettable experience.

> 'Visitors often tell me that the organ music was superb, but then they ask where the organ is hidden and I have to own up.'
>
> 'I have all the best organists in the world playing in this church.'
>
> 'We put the control desk in the old organ loft and I sit up there and run the show. As I reached the foot of the stairs one week after a service, a couple of visitors stopped me to congratulate me on my organ playing.'

Even those who sell such packages will tell you that they are not as good as the real thing. They can be inflexible and perhaps mechanical, but to many congregations they are a lifeline. We should remember that in the past barrel devices were used to play the organ in churches: those offered less flexibility than the modern-day equivalent.

Using CDs you can build a reasonable library for £50, but bear in mind that a sound system, even in a small church, will need to be more powerful than a domestic unit. It is possible to use CDs with accompaniment and singing, and in some churches that might be advantageous as a small congregation will not feel too exposed. You can also obtain CDs with accompaniment only, and many internet sites offer such an option. Perhaps that option should provide the most authentic alternative to live music, but there will be some drawbacks. The most obvious will be that the pre-recorded CD will not always offer the right number of verses for your hymn book. There will also be no flexibility in terms of pitch so that some hymns may prove to be too high or too low for your particular use. The tempo is also fixed, and some may prefer it to be faster or slower. However, these drawbacks can also exist with some organists.

CD packages are also available offering worship group performances.

> 'Call me old-fashioned but I do like to sing the hymn that I've announced and with the right number of verses.'

You can introduce some more flexibility with an MP3 package. For this you will need to connect a computer or tablet to your sound system. There are advantages in terms of handling. A complete playlist for a service can be set up with everything in the right order to avoid playing the wrong track on the wrong CD, but it also takes time to prepare. The sound quality from MP3s is often not as good as from a CD, and this may well be more noticeable when amplified. To most people, though, the difference will be minimal.

MIDI files are also available and can be played on a computer connected to a sound system or on most modern keyboard devices. MIDI files can be difficult to handle, and once again preparation is important – as indeed it would be with live musicians.

Then there are electronic hymnals – preprogrammed, specialist MIDI file players, usually preset with a generous range of hymns. With these devices you can set up the hymns for a service and arrange the number of verses, the pitch, the speed and other features. They are highly versatile machines and the remote control can add to the attraction. The cost might not be so attractive.

> 'Our chapels have these preprogrammed devices, and they sensibly have a book by the side of the machine, and once a hymn is sung, they make a note of tempo/level of sound that was deemed comfortable etc. in preparation for the next time it is used.'

Being able to preprogramme a device can be a huge advantage, but it can also be a disadvantage when you need a few hymns in a hurry. The answer should be in forward planning but we, like you, live in the real world.

Earlier we mentioned the barrel devices that fitted organ keyboards and with a turn of the handle enabled the organ to be played. Actually, this was often extremely labour intensive, as you not only needed a gentle hand on the barrel apparatus but also needed another hand on the organ pumping device and a further hand to operate the organ stops. At least two of the three were seldom in reach of another. There is now a UK company that offers an electronic barrel device that can be fitted to the organ keyboard and will play the keys. There is no little handle to turn either. Inspiration is provided from MIDI files.

If you enter the world of pre-recorded music it may offer you another opportunity. Perhaps you can find a member of the congregation or a student from a local school who would be keen to take on the programming process.

Observant clergy will have already noted that, given a sound system and a few CDs, they could have complete control over the music in the service. But who would they then have to argue with?

Finally, plainsong hymns were originally sung without accompaniment. Singing at football stadiums is also accomplished without accompaniment. Unaccompanied singing can still work very well.

> 'Our small congregation are happy to sing the hymns unaccompanied and do so very well.'

FOUR

The changing face

The style and form of congregational singing is by no means the only change in the music of our churches. A recent (2013) survey carried out for a County Organists' Association provides some interesting information, even though the catchment was restricted to the Church of England in that county. Of 460 questionnaires that were delivered to the clergy, 329 were returned – roughly 71 per cent.

Of those responding, 97 per cent of churches had organs, of which 84 per cent were pipe organs, 12 per cent were electronic and 4 per cent were harmoniums.

Ninety-nine per cent of the organs were declared playable, although only 93 per cent were the subject of regular tuning and maintenance; 'regular' may in some cases mean annual.

Around 69 per cent of churches had a regular organist, while 18 per cent used a rota and 13 per cent had no organist. Approximately 55 per cent of organists were reported as being in the age range 61–80, with 13 per cent of organists being over 80.

Sixty-six per cent of churches used no other instruments than an organ, while 16 per cent used an electronic keyboard, 15 per cent used a piano, 15 per cent used a guitar, 11 per cent used woodwind instruments, 6 per cent used a drum kit, 6 per cent used stringed instruments, 2 per cent used other instruments and one church used a barrel organ.

Around 22.5 per cent of churches had a choir; 72 per cent of choirs reported an average age of members as over 60, and only 3 per cent of choirs could boast an average age of between 20 and 40.

Only five churches did not use hymns. Worship songs were used in 134 churches, psalms and canticles were sung in 86, anthems were sung in 68, choruses were sung in 63 and Taizé chants were used in 52.

While giving a very useful picture of those actively engaged in church music-making in a shire county, the picture may not be typical of the whole country, particularly the larger conurbations, nor typical of all denominations. It would be helpful if similar organisations could undertake such investigations in their own areas.

> 'I'm getting on for 90 but I know that when I go that will be it. This dear old organ is just about as rickety as me. They won't keep it once I'm gone.'

In the last 20 years organs have begun to vanish from some churches. If the organ needs a potentially expensive major overhaul, if there is no organist regularly available, if there is doubt that potential members of the congregation find the sound of an organ attractive, then small wonder if the organ is removed.

These are not joyful tidings, and might represent the end of an era. That era began in some churches when the members of the West Gallery band were given their marching orders because of the introduction of the very instrument that is now seen to be in decline. In some churches it must feel as though the wheel has come full circle, as the organ has been replaced by a worship band.

Yet the wheel hasn't quite come full circle. The West Gallery band was, as its name implies, at the west end of the church, behind the congregation. Most worship bands are in front of the congregation, often centre stage – and stage is the word used – with the words projected on a screen above the band who are facing the congregation. The sound of the band will usually be amplified. Anyone entering such a church for the first time is bound to ask where the main focus of the community's faith lies.

If your church is contemplating a band or music group, take as much care and time over the positioning of the band as you would over the installation of a toilet and kitchen facility or the reordering of the church. Where should the band be in relation to the altar, for example? In which direction should the band be facing? Think about the role of the band. Is it to accompany the congregation or to offer a musical moment to encourage the worshippers in their prayer, praise and meditation? Ask what level of sound is appropriate.

Worship bands

> 'Oh yes, I admit that we use some of the modern hymns. Many of them are very effective.'
>
> 'Sometimes the children bring percussion instruments into church from the junior church.'
>
> 'My congregation does not want to repeat three words over and over.'

Like organs and organists, the quality of worship bands can vary greatly. In one church it is difficult not to be impressed by the musical skills of the players and by the very professional presentation techniques used to enhance a performance. In another church a guitarist who struggles to change from one chord to another, together with a drummer who is certainly loud but not always in time, do little if anything to enhance worship. They are not assisted in the challenge by a scratchy violinist and an out-of-tune flautist. The rediscovery of the priesthood of all believers may have encouraged all who played an instrument to join the band, but it doesn't always result in an uplifting musical performance.

In recent years, however, there has been a move towards regaining the highest standards in musical worship and striving for excellence, not only in terms of performance but also in the quality of instruments, lighting, sound and production. All this enables those familiar with a consumer and high-tech society to recognise in church what they are familiar with in the world at large.

Undoubtedly, the introduction of worship bands in church has not always been comfortable for the more elderly members of some congregations, who still feel an allegiance to 'their' church and are ill at ease with the new forms of worship and music that are alien to their experience. Conversation and discussion among all the church members is as vital as ever in a new era.

That conversation needs to acknowledge the substantial changes that have taken place in many churches. As ministers began to stand behind the altar facing west, and altars have been brought forward into the nave of the church, so the church has developed an understanding of itself as a fellowship of believers. As the words of the creed have changed from 'I believe' to 'We believe', so individual members of the congregation have seen themselves as members of the body of Christ. The words of hymns and worship songs reflect this growing sense of fellowship, many of which offer encouragement to fellow worshippers and emphasise the importance of the worshipping community. A cursory glance at the 'We . . .' section in the index of a songbook suggests that many songs, rather than being directed to God, are directed to the worshipping community. The music and accompaniment of these songs also attempt to bring worshippers together into a committed, Spirit-filled community.

Questions for discussion

- Would it be useful to draw together a small group to examine the health of the present musical tradition in your church?
- What productive outcomes might there be from a discussion or talk on the development of musical traditions within your denomination?
- What might be the advantages of researching the musical history of your church?
- What might be the advantages of using the outcomes of such research as a starting point for discussion about the way forward if it is felt that music in your church is reaching the end of an era?

Worship music

The influence of worship music from the 1970s onwards is felt across many different forms of worship. Christians who do not feel totally at home within the contemporary worship tradition nevertheless admit to using its material in their own services.

When Isaac Watts wrote his hymn 'When I survey the wondrous cross', such personal testimony in hymns was relatively unusual. Today the expression of a personal relationship with God gives rise to a more intimate approach in the writing of hymns and songs. This repertoire has come from individuals and an urgency to write for a particular worshipping community. The songs have found their way into the wider community, often by way of the internet, and many have been widely adopted.

Some will argue that contemporary worship songs are light on theology and heavy on feelings. They are repetitious and have not stood the test of time. They are full of clichés and devoid of literary excellence. On the other hand, others suggest that classical hymnody is too wordy and theologically weighty to reach the heart. The language and music are outdated and inaccessible.

Yet the text of the Communion and the Mass contains very few words. The 'Hallelujah chorus' is repetitive. Some of the most popular hymns like 'Great is thy faithfulness' and 'How great thou art' are certainly not devoid of theological content. Hymn writers must also be given a chance. After all, songwriters like Gershwin and Berlin, who wrote some of the most popular songs that are still sung today, wrote thousands of songs with their contemporaries on Tin Pan Alley. Most of those songs didn't last. So too, the hymns that we sing by Charles Wesley are but a tiny fraction of his total output. Most of his hymns didn't last. We must expect and allow a new style of worship song to develop in a similar way.

The worship leader

With contemporary church music a new musical role has emerged, and is continuing to develop.

> 'The role of a worship leader in leading the music is different from that of an organist, choirmaster or even director of music in the older tradition.'

In some ways, the new role has more direct influence.

> 'The worship leader not only decides what the songs will be but often also makes more radical decisions about what kind of setting a particular song will have and how the music will be used to influence the course of the worship.'

Worship leaders have great influence within the service itself, deciding how many times a song is going to be repeated or perhaps doubling back to an earlier verse. Such decisions may be made in outline in advance, but some may well also be made 'as the Spirit moves' in the inspiration of the moment. If the worship leader feels that the congregation is beginning to engage with a song, they may decide that it is worth 'taking it round again'. The congregation may not just sing from the first verse to the end but will follow the lead of the band and singers. The projection of the words can assist in that process. Perhaps the worship leader, in the course of introducing a song, will direct the attention of the congregation to a particular aspect of the text or the music.

With that position of influence comes huge responsibility. There is clear potential for tensions between the minister or priest and the worship leader.

> 'Having witnessed words being projected onto the screen, the difficulty arises where the worship leader "goes with the Spirit" but the person operating the laptop and projector is not in tune and therefore words and pages jump around until they have caught up with the band – leaving some within the congregation somewhat confused.'

In some services, the organisation of the music will be unfamiliar. Sometimes the music will fall into blocks rather than hymns punctuating readings, sermons and prayers. Where this is so, there might well be a preparatory or gathering block, reinforcing the reason why the worshippers are meeting. Later in the service there will be another block, the role of which could be to reinforce the message of readings or prayers, and finally there will be a block working on from the theme and moving towards 'sending out'.

> 'Having the band has put new life into our worship.'
>
> 'She asked me if I would like to play in the band and I jumped at the chance.'

The composition of the band can vary greatly. It could include drums, bass guitar, lead and rhythm guitars, keyboards, flute, clarinet and almost anything else. Melody instruments will often all play from the vocal line, and that may involve making extempore transpositions for B♭ instruments, octave transpositions for flutes, etc. Improvisation skills also play an important part, with many of the musicians welcoming the opportunity to improvise their way either around the original melody or the original chord sequence. At times the harmony will be stripped to a bare minimum, at others it will be enriched, and in performance during the service the band will need to be reactive to the nuances and signals emanating from the worship leader. Keyboard players will need to possess the skills to enable them to read from the 'dots' or from chord symbols. The drummer may not read music – indeed, there may be no music available. Crucial decisions will have to be made at rehearsals which will take on a new importance, with a group of musicians being involved rather than perhaps just an organist.

> 'I reckon I am as serious about rehearsal as the old choirmasters used to be.'

Preparation for rehearsals is also vital. Worship leaders will work from a variety of sources. Printed music will be important, but so will performances found on the internet. Such performances could hugely influence the 'orchestration' and manner of performance.

More than just the music

> 'It's not just the music now. Everything has to fit together and play its part.'

Much of the recorded music currently available from various resources such as the internet and CDs relies on production techniques and subtle musical skills for its effect. A performance on guitar and voice will not create that effect, and that poses problems for many musicians in churches that cannot boast the full range of equipment together with the production and musical expertise found in abundance in larger churches. It can also lead to tensions where the expectations of the local priest or minister may not take into account the constraints of local circumstances.

Questions for discussion

- Which features of the working method outlined above might be useful to consider in planning worship in your church?
- What advantages might accrue, for preaching and prayers as well as for music, from adopting a more collaborative method of planning and preparing services for your church?

Resources

> 'A year ago I didn't know what an app was. Now we are experimenting with one to give us our music.'

Where the resources are not available there are alternatives. There are apps that provide backings linked to on-screen projections and, although they limit flexibility, they can be effective. Even so, the outlay on good quality sound, lighting and projection could induce more than a tremor in the church treasurer. At that point it may be well worthwhile to remind the treasurer about the cost of repairing the organ.

The changing face?

The common factor in all this is no longer simply the denomination of the church. It is often the will to move the music towards a different dimension that cuts across denominations and traditions.

Many of the common problems and irritations sadly travel only too well. Worship leaders and organists/choirmasters alike have often become targets of criticism from the clergy regarding the element of musical performance taking precedence over the service as a whole.

> 'I believe he thinks that we have a rock concert here every Sunday morning.'

The changing face of music within our churches is not unique. The greater desire for fellowship is reflected in the reordering of our churches and the provision of areas for social gathering facilitating coffee and conversation after the service. Messy Church and Café Church have also made demands upon the use of church buildings. Yet when considering the reordering of ancient churches, we will employ the best architects known for their sensitivity to historic buildings. When relighting our buildings or installing sound systems, we look for professional help. Many church buildings require us, legally, to employ professional expertise. Of course, we look for experts who have some experience of working with church congregations, but we still expect them to tease out the use we want to make of our building, our aims and hopes for our fellowship.

When it comes to music, we are often hesitant to think of employing the services of a professional consultant. The successful reordering of so many of our churches to make them fit for twenty-first-century use should encourage us to seek the same standard of help for the music.

FIVE

Service music

'I would love to see a greater theological awareness in church musicians, especially when they choose the music for services.'

'It would be good if those who choose the music realised that one style will not suit everybody.'

'Does music have to serve the worship or can it have a leading role?'

'We are so tied up with tradition.'

'Our main challenge is to develop a musical style that will deepen the congregation's experience during worship.'

'The main problem for us is balancing the traditional and the contemporary.'

'We use more difficult choir settings at Christmas and other festivals. It gives the choir a challenge.'

While the music in our churches is often found within an informal worship setting, formal liturgy remains an important, if not the main, form of service in many churches. Our hopes for music in worship to create fellowship and a sense of the presence of God, to focus our attention on the actions of the Eucharist and help us experience its power, will have an influence upon communion settings, psalms and canticles, anthems and voluntaries, as well as upon hymns and congregational songs.

The function of congregational service music will vary in different denominations and churches. In some churches the same setting will be sung each week. The justification might be that the congregation feels comfortable with that setting. Even so, researching the views of the congregation might provide a few surprises. Some might well welcome change and variety whereas, to others, such change and variety might just be confusing and counter-productive. Some members of the congregation might even tell you that they would be upset by change.

In some churches the strong tradition relating to service music can be a positive thing. But tradition grows and evolves, and even what happened last Sunday becomes part of the tradition in a small way.

Some churches add significance to the church liturgical calendar by selecting service music that is felt to be most suitable to that particular season.

Working with a choir

There is a difference between a choir setting and a congregational setting. If you have a choir they will relish the challenge of working on a choir setting, and they might well become stale and miserable without such a challenge. There is an understandable tendency towards using a more elaborate musical menu on high days and holy days. But does it make sense to use complicated settings that are more suited to the choir at Christmas, for example, when some of those attending are fairly unused to church? If it is their only visit in the year it might not matter, as most of the service will be unfamiliar. But members of the congregation, especially visitors, value the opportunity to join in with familiar music at the key points in the church year.

It may well be profitable to consider a special 'choir service' where most of the music can provide challenges for the choir.

Anthems

> 'The choir make a bit of a din. It can be embarrassing.'
>
> 'I look forward to being invited to take a service in your church because listening to the choir is always so wonderful.'
>
> 'In Quires and Places where they sing, here followeth the anthem.'
>
> 'Do you find music sung out of tune very uplifting?'

It would indeed be heartening if the second quotation above were to be applied to your church. It came from the opening of the sermon delivered by a visiting preacher. So perhaps the first consideration is, can they sing, or will it be embarrassing? If the latter, then careful choice of repertoire could still enable an ageing choir to make a positive contribution to the worship. One of the purposes of singing an anthem is often to encourage the choir in their musical endeavours.

Listening to an anthem can be a fairly passive activity for members of the congregation. Some will have well-developed listening skills and will find a focus easily, but to others the musical language will be so far removed from the sort of music they treasure that absorbing the content and even being moved by it will be impossible.

> 'I thought one Sunday, I wonder what they made of that? Then I thought – strangely – that is the first time I've ever considered it. It set me on a path to considering what the congregation actually do during the anthem and how I could enable them to be less passive and more actively involved.'

Some members of the congregation will be very happy to allow the music to wash over them and transport them in their thoughts and reflections. Others might be more stimulated if they could see a copy of the words of the anthem. Some perhaps would not think that the words were important at all.

> 'You can never hear the words they are singing.'

Regularity of performance and linkage to the material of the service seem to be important factors.

> 'I think most of the choir would like to sing by themselves in each service, but I believe the vicar has other ideas.'
>
> 'She gives me a note with the title of the anthem. I have to admit that I'm not musical so it means very little to me. I've encouraged her to add a few words to open up the context.'
>
> 'Sometimes the spirit of the anthem seems far removed from the focus for the rest of the service.'

Choosing varied repertoire and styles

> 'We have a monthly Taizé service which has a regular following.'
>
> 'The men from the choir sing Compline to plainsong, as part of Evensong, four times a year.'
>
> 'From time to time we use plainsong for the psalms.'
>
> 'In using Gelineau settings we can encourage congregational participation in the antiphons which we use after each verse.'
>
> 'Even though we have no organ, we have a strong singer to sing the verses, and the congregation respond with the antiphon.'
>
> 'At Evensong the congregation sits while the choir sings the psalms to Anglican chants.'
>
> 'I don't believe it is possible for the congregation to join in singing psalms to Anglican chants so we don't do it.'
>
> 'We read alternate verses of psalms.'

It is possible to spoil lovely friendships by discussing the effectiveness of congregations singing Anglican chants! Following adequate rehearsal and with a musician who has a consistent view of methodology, the effect of a choir performance can be very moving. Such an effect is not easy to achieve if you involve the congregation without rehearsal, especially if they don't even have marked copies. Even with marked copies clearly indicating the pointing, most members of the congregation who have a mind to join in might be more preoccupied with following the pointing indicators rather than gaining much from the words. It can be an illuminating experience to ask cathedral choir members, who perform the psalms regularly, about the meaning and significance of the words. They are often dedicated to the sounds that the words make, but meaning and significance can be the 'one that got away'.

> 'I find sitting and listening to a fine performance of a psalm a wonderful musical experience. But we don't have a choir so we use performances from a variety of cathedrals on CD. It gives us all time to reflect on what we have just read.'

Psalm settings that incorporate repeated antiphons allow both the choir and the congregation to play an active part. The Gelineau settings are a fine example and deserve more frequent use. The congregation also have the opportunity to ponder the words of the verses sung, perhaps by a choir or soloist, between their contributions in the antiphon.

Voluntaries

'Whatever the proficiency of the player or the resources of the instrument, what does matter is that voluntaries are chosen with care, bearing in mind their suitability to any given occasion.'[9]

> 'I am fed up playing voluntaries. The congregation could not care less and just walk out.'
>
> 'There is a tradition in our church that the congregation sits and listens to the voluntary after the service.'
>
> 'One of our ministers calls it "the treat" after the service.'
>
> 'I like to send them home with their ears ringing.'
>
> 'I always choose to play something rousing.'
>
> 'It is no good if you send them home feeling miserable.'
>
> 'Our organist plays so loudly after the service you cannot hear yourself speak.'

I wonder why the congregation 'could not care less and just walk out'. It could perhaps be that the voluntary is usually similar in style and

---

9. Lionel Dakers, *Parish Music* (Norwich: The Canterbury Press, 1991), p.33.

character and has become wallpaper. If you 'always choose to play something rousing', perhaps that is too predictable. And perhaps they do not always want to be sent 'home with their ears ringing'. If it really is to be 'the treat', it needs to be varied, and an effective way to achieve that is to plan the voluntary around the theme of the service or around the church season. Sometimes it will be just as effective to provide a voluntary that makes a strong contrast to what has gone before. In either case, it would be advantageous for musicians and clergy to work closely together in order to enable the musicians to understand more clearly the aim or theme of the service and perhaps try out a few ideas for music that might add to its effectiveness.

Questions for discussion

- Does the voluntary after the service always have to be loud?
- Does the voluntary after the service always have to be lively?
- Can the voluntary after the service sometimes be reflective?
- Can the voluntary after the service sometimes be calming?
- Does reflective music imply 'send[ing] them home feeling miserable'?
- How might you find out what members of the congregation enjoy as music after a service?
- Should you always play their choices?
- Do you try to provide a varied diet of music after the service each week or are you inclined to play music of a similar period and style?
- Might it be useful to keep a record of music that you have played at different churches?
- Might it be effective to repeat a voluntary, perhaps through the Sundays of a particular season?

One of the reasons why people walk out during the voluntary is that our culture is conditioned to using music simply as background to other activities. The assumption is not that here is something to listen to as part of the service but that here is a signal to leave. Choosing the voluntary because of its relevance to the service might be a first step, but it will not prevent an exodus by itself. It may take some time to establish a practice that the voluntary is in fact part of the service and that people are encouraged to listen to it. Suggestions to that effect can be made, either in service sheets or by the minister or priest. Better still, they can come from interested members of the congregation. It is a matter of establishing a culture, and that will take time.

Length could be another factor. It might not be realistic to expect the congregation to sit for a further ten minutes after a long service.

If worshippers are encouraged to sit and listen to the voluntary after the service, the clergy will be giving an odd message if they get up and walk out.

> 'Before the service they just sit and chat, and perhaps that is a good thing for them, but it makes playing music fairly soul-destroying.'
>
> 'I don't really like playing while the bells are ringing.'
>
> 'Prior to the service, I try to play some hymn preludes based on hymns that we shall share later in the service.'
>
> 'I've built up a list of music suitable for the main events in the church year. Each Advent I start again.'
>
> 'She never plays anything that is not right for the particular service.'
>
> 'I try to "bring the congregation down" from chatter and clatter to an atmosphere more fitting to worship.'

Music before a service was, at one time, usually restrained in nature, but fashions change. Predictability is not necessarily a strong ally, and it is certainly not guaranteed to attract the attention your performance deserves. Linking with hymns, particularly those that are not particularly well known, is a very useful practice, and the organist who describes his plan to 'bring the congregation down' clearly has a structure and purpose in mind. It might be worthwhile sharing that purpose with the congregation.

The music before a service inevitably accompanies people arriving and walking around the church before taking their places. If it is felt important to add significance and make more of that musical offering, then a welcome by the priest or minister when all have arrived, followed by an indication that quiet will be kept as a preparation for worship while a voluntary is played, could be an effective practice to establish.

An article in the magazine might spark some interest. It could be useful to share views on the purpose of music before and after the service, and that would involve seeking the views of the readers.

Playing over the efforts of the team of bell-ringers is not the favourite occupation of many organists, but some tell us that there is a particular 'frisson' in listening to organ and bells in different keys.

> 'I publish the titles of my voluntaries, both pre- and post-service, on the service sheet. Sometimes I even add some explanation as well.'
>
> 'I sometimes ask for something about a voluntary after the service to be included in the notices.'

One organist has a picture frame on the table by the entrance to the church. Each week he inserts the title and composer of the voluntary in the hope of informing the congregation. Others undertake a similar practice by including the information in the service sheets or on the projector screen. At least one church arranges for photos on the screen to accompany the music. That could be a challenge, and doubtless it could spawn some controversy. Some colleagues would suggest that it is better just to let the music speak for itself.

A section of the church website devoted to music could be helpful to members of the congregation in many ways. It could certainly enable them to begin to relate more effectively to the musical material of voluntaries. It is not always easy to decide what information to give. It could be worthwhile to consider what members of your particular congregation will make of just a title and composer.

> 'I'm not really up to voluntaries and I doubt I ever will be, so I play over a couple of suitable hymns, and I've pinched an idea from a colleague who showed me how to just play around the tune a bit.'

> 'I went to this really useful event where some organists brought along some hymn preludes and played them. I picked up some lovely pieces that I had never heard or played before.'

> 'Our organists' association is setting up an event where we each play a favourite voluntary and share the source with our fellow members.'

You don't have to be a brilliant organist in order to play effective music and perhaps even make it your own. Sharing inspiration with other organists will be particularly useful to those who are building up a repertoire. Whatever technical standard you are capable of, preparation is all.

> 'There is nothing clever in an "on the spur of the moment" choice which can lead to dire sounds being inflicted on the listeners.'[10]

> 'Well, you can't really go wrong with Bach, can you?'

No comment.

10. Lionel Dakers, *Parish Music*, p.33.

Worship music

> 'We have ongoing problems and arguments around use of different musical genres.'
>
> 'The word "tradition" is often quoted.'
>
> 'The organist became so laid back that we moved towards having a music group.'
>
> 'The music group is a delight and easy to work with. They join forces with the organ at times.'
>
> 'We started a music group but even that has no young members.'
>
> 'We have a young pianist who leads family worship and is putting a worship group together.'
>
> 'We have three services: the first is traditional but uses recorded music, the second uses a guitar and the third uses a band.'
>
> 'I'm a fan of the music group but they don't suit all the songs we want to sing and they can be very loud at times.'

Perhaps some services in your church benefit from being led by a worship group offering an alternative dimension that is lacking in the traditional choir and organ partnership. Perhaps there are some features that such a group might have to offer which a choir and organ lack. Many traditional church musicians struggle with the notion that there may be another way of 'doing' the music in church. The clergy have a difficult path to tread, requiring tact and diplomacy to change hearts and minds; many such attempts end in tears and recriminations. The resulting acrimony does little to present an attractive picture of Christian worship to outsiders.

The potential for attracting younger people into the congregation must be difficult to ignore if you minister to a diminishing congregation who are all over the age of 70. You might find that, if you have some success, you produce two distinct congregations. Many churches have found that the two congregations get on rather well, with particular success in harmonious coexistence between old and young. The two camps of musicians might find peaceful relations more difficult to handle. Matters can easily become fraught when a well-established pattern, which works on the principle of different times, different places, different styles, breaks down because 'next week is Easter'.

There is a view that introducing worship music will make it easier to attract 'young people'. That may not be the case at all. Very often the favoured musical style of the sought-after 'young people' is far removed from that of the worship band. In comparison with their favourite band, a worship group will not be hugely attractive simply because they do not have the 'sound' of the favourite band. That said, the music of the young is unlikely to be a close relative of the more traditional style of church music.

Once again, we should not be afraid to ask for help. One church asked young musicians to play a suitable piece during the administration of communion on one Sunday in the month. It presented a different experience from the choir and the organ, and it gave the youngsters the opportunity to play in a wonderful acoustic. There are many composers who would relish the opportunity to work with a congregation on a communion setting or anthem for a special occasion. Many cathedrals employ artists in residence. Such an idea is possible on a smaller scale and can provide valuable links with the community.

SIX

Choirs

Choirs have always played an important role in religious worship. Indeed, choirs may well have originated within a religious context. In the Old Testament there is a vivid description of the musical forces enhancing the worship of the temple.

> All the Levitical singers, Asaph, Heman, and Jeduthun, their sons and kindred, arrayed in fine linen, with cymbals, harps, and lyres, stood east of the altar with one hundred and twenty priests who were trumpeters, it was the duty of the trumpeters and singers to make themselves heard in unison in praise and thanksgiving to the Lord, and when the song was raised, with trumpets and cymbals and other musical instruments, in praise to the Lord,
> 'For he is good,
> for his steadfast love endures forever',
> the house, the house of the Lord, was filled with a cloud, so that the priests could not stand to minister because of the cloud; for the glory of the Lord filled the house of God.
>
> *2 Chronicles 5:12-14*

It must have been a stupendous sound, with the men singing in unison and the fanfares from 120 trumpets!

Musicians have always wanted to exploit great buildings for dramatic musical effect. When Nehemiah celebrated the rebuilding of the walls of Jerusalem, he did so not with one but two choirs:

> Then I brought the leaders of Judah up on to the wall, and appointed two great companies that gave thanks and went in procession. One went to the right on the wall to the Dung Gate; and after them went Hoshaiah and half the officials of Judah, and Azariah, Ezra, Meshullam, Judah, Benjamin, Shemaiah, and Jeremiah, and some of the young priests with trumpets: Zechariah son of Jonathan son of Shemaiah son of Mattaniah son of Micaiah son of Zaccur son of Asaph . . .
>
> *Nehemiah 12:31-35*

Some 2000 years later, music by Gabrieli, Monteverdi and Schutz, utilising choirs disposed in different areas of the building, thrilled the congregations of St Mark's in Venice. It may seem a world away from a small English rural parish church with its chancel choir stalls, now empty, and curtained vestry at the back of the church where choir robes and psalters gather dust.

Choirs come in all shapes and sizes, from the small group of professional singers, no more than one or two to a part, without accompaniment, inspiring worship in the Orthodox church, to the gospel choir rocking the congregation of the Baptist city church.

The form that any church choir takes will be governed by its purposes, which may be many and varied, and may include:

- enriching the worship;
- encouraging others to sing;
- enabling singers to use their talents to praise God;
- allowing time for reflection on the words of Scripture or the liturgy;
- attracting others to faith and worship;
- educating its members in faith and music;
- supporting its members socially and spiritually.

Vladimir the Great, the tenth-century prince of Kiev, wanted to find a religion to bind his people together. According to the story, he sent out envoys to experience the different faiths. On their return, Vladimir didn't like their reports of Islamic and Jewish dietary restrictions but was impressed by the dazzling worship his ambassadors described seeing in the great Cathedral of Hagia Sophia in Constantinople. Their words were along these lines:

> 'We knew not whether we were in heaven or on earth, for surely there is no such splendour or beauty anywhere upon earth. We cannot describe it to you. Only we know that God dwells there among men, and that their service surpasses the worship of all other places. We cannot forget that beauty.'

> 'A choir! We haven't had one of those for quite some years.'
>
> 'We would like to revive the choir but need someone with the skills to do so and who could make the commitment.'
>
> 'The choir members are also very busy in their lives so we suffer from lack of numbers at times.'
>
> 'Our choir has a holiday one Sunday in each month when we have a family service.'
>
> 'Men in the choir – you must be joking!'
>
> 'The current age and entrenched views of the choir make progress difficult.'
>
> 'I am trying to address the quality of the singing.'
>
> 'It has been very encouraging to see the choir grow and develop a more significant role in recent years.'

A thought

In writing this book we have returned many times to contemplating the irony that, while many towns are spawning 'Gareth Malone'-type choirs with waiting lists of members, many church choirs, perhaps even in the same towns, are struggling to stay alive. We have questioned why it is not possible to start a new choir, along Gareth Malone lines, that would sing both in the community and in church. We have asked what attracts people to such choirs, and have wondered whether it would be possible to use that attraction to advantage. We offer the thought that ministers, priests and musicians might find potential benefit in making contact and entering into dialogue with the leaders of such choirs.

> 'There is a classic situation in one of my churches: our choir is declining in numbers, but the building is host to FOUR community choirs during the week.'

Might we perhaps also need to give some thought to the product that we have on offer?

Recruiting

> 'There are no young people in the choir.'
>
> 'Several families brought their children to church so we have started a children's choir.'
>
> 'We found a new leader for our choir and it has gone from four members all over 70 to eight young members.'
>
> 'We need youth to lead our worship.'
>
> 'We need to re-establish work with children.'

What image comes to mind when you hear the phrase 'church choir'? Is it a service of Nine Lessons and Carols or a cathedral choir of men and boys? Perhaps it's a few elderly folk, the men in robes that don't fit and the women wearing rather peculiar hats. Or is it a lively, dancing gospel choir? Simply inviting people to join the church choir may conjure up all kinds of misleading images. In some cases, it may be better to avoid the word 'choir' altogether and concentrate on the church's aspirations for enhancing the worship with music and the benefits to the church of having a group of singers.

If recruiting from scratch, it may be best to start with one particular event, gathering people together to sing at a carol service, for example. A singing day or a Come and Sing could promote the joys and benefits of singing: the concentration and challenge which energise people at the end of a long working week provide a wonderful release and opportunity to express thoughts and feelings, and give regular opportunity for singing for those who haven't the time to sing on their own, with all the benefits of a social and community activity.

Questions for discussion

When approaching people to join the choir:

- will they go away believing that the future of the choir depends on them?
- will they go away believing that they have the unique skills and experience that the choir needs?
- will you tell them first what they could do for the choir or what the choir could do for them?

We might deprecate the reality of living in a society that needs to know 'what's in it for me?' It can work positively for us, though. If you are clear about the benefits that could accrue from singing in your choir you are likely to set out to recruit new members with a positive attitude, and potential members will be engaged to learn what your choir can do for them. It may well be useful for clergy and musicians to share ideas about the positive value of being a choir member.

> 'Choir-trainers are often too modest about what they can offer children. Many parents will encourage their children to join anything they feel will do the children good, if they are convinced that it is worthwhile.'[11]

Questions for discussion:

Do you believe and publicise:

- the potential for discovering how to listen carefully by singing in a choir?
- that when singing in a choir you have to listen, so that your voice blends with the voice of the person next to you?
- that by singing in a choir you can discover how to monitor your sound based on how it feels?
- that you can take the opportunity to work on your ear by singing in a choir?
- that picking out your part when the other voices of the choir are surrounding you is a good workout for your ear?
- that by singing in a choir you might find a chance to work on your social skills?

---

11. Lionel Dakers, *Parish Music*, p.53.

- that in a choir you might find people who like similar music to you, or are inspired by beautiful music?
- that by singing with others, you may find that your anxieties about performing dissolve?
- that if you feel comfortable within a group, you may be able to transfer that comfort level to your solo singing?
- that singing in a choir is FUN?

There are spiritual as well as musical benefits to singing in a choir. Not all ministers and priests seem to be aware of these. The repetition involved in rehearsal gives opportunity for reflection on biblical and spiritual texts. Contributing to worship involves being sensitive to the drama involved. The listening, learning, criticism and cooperation demanded by choral singing also require patience and humility. And like all community activities, there must be support, care and encouragement by choir members for each other.

Most who sing would probably agree that singing is a wonderful release and a great opportunity to express thoughts and feelings through music. It is also possible that the challenge and joy of singing in a group may be just the lift needed at the end of a long week of work.

> 'We have singers who will help us with large, special services and some weddings, but they will not commit to a regular service every Sunday.'

Does a choir have to be assembled for every week of the year? There might be purpose in drawing together a choir for special services and events.

> 'At a previous church we organised a Singing Group to plan one-off events. The age range and ability were broad, but it worked extremely well as folk opted in to a short-term commitment. A further benefit was that items from the group were then fed into subsequent services, but as congregational items where the singers were dispersed and offered a lead. It worked extremely well.'

A fundamental marketing strategy in any field of activity is targeting. Profiling of likely targets and identifying where and on whom to focus is likely to result in successful recruitment of new choir members.

Questions for discussion

- What neighbourhoods might reward being targeted?
- What type of events do those you might want to target attend?

- Where might they spend their free time?
- Would that be where you should target first? For example, one choir found a rich harvest from flyers left in coffee shops.

These questions imply the need to go out and seek new members. Sometimes it seems that we wait for new members to come into church.

The potential members that you find may need help and support to become active members of the choir. As an example, how could you help a young couple who both would like to sing but need a babysitter? It might be possible to persuade a couple of partners of regular choir members to run a crèche. A more informal arrangement with babysitters could be easier to arrange and would involve less red tape. It is likely that clergy know the potential areas and families where recruiting could be of benefit.

Who does the recruiting is also an important consideration. Young people are more likely to attract young people; older folk more likely to attract their peers. Recruiting shouldn't be left to the organist or choir trainer. It is much better if the minister or priest and musicians work together and with existing choir members.

How about challenging the choir each to find a new member? One choir tried this and were pleasantly surprised by the outcome.

Auditions

> 'Oh no, we don't do that. If they want to sing they are in and we repent at leisure.'
>
> 'I would not know where to begin.'
>
> 'I don't believe it is possible to maintain any standard of singing unless potential singers face an audition.'

Perhaps you use an audition for potential new choir members. Asking a person already confident in singing to take an audition might not cause too much concern, but the same process with someone trying to enter the singing world for the first time and not yet really comfortable about using their voice can be intimidating. One of us remembers his first choir where, always with a smile, in the bass section stood Mr T, who sang everything on a monotone. He'd fooled the previous organist by telling him about choirs in which he had previously sung.

Some choirs hold a more informal audition, telling the singer that the purpose is to find out what their voice can do and how it can best be of value to the choir.

Perhaps you have a waiting list to join your choir. On the other hand, some choirs are very pleased to grab any interested party who can remain vertical and breathing for more than 30 seconds.

It is an advantage if you are clear about the aptitude and level of skill that you will be looking for in a choir member at audition. Perhaps you will be seeking:

- a voice that will blend;
- a voice that can be worked on;
- a finished voice.

All three could be an advantage from the point of view of a choir. If we return to 'what's in it for the singer', then the prospect of receiving support and guidance in developing their voice could be a strong incentive. It is important that the potential member believes that they will learn to improve their singing through the choir.

Having selected your criteria against which to audition applicants, it might be worthwhile asking whether they should be the same for every applicant or whether there could be any advantage in trying to match some criteria to the individual.

If you ask the applicant to sing a scale, might you learn different things about their voice from an ascending and a descending scale? What might you learn:

- from singing their head register downwards?
- from singing their chest register upwards?

If they are not aware of either register, how could you take them there?

Depending on repertoire, some choirs will treasure a strong chest register whereas others will seek to expand the head register downwards.

If you ask the applicant to sing a short solo for audition, you could select the solo, but it will allow for greater confidence if you ask them to perform a piece of their own choice, albeit perhaps not something from the repertoire of the choir.

Finding pitch from a piano or organ can be daunting if you are not used to doing so; it is often much easier to find pitch from another voice. That will, after all, be the reality of singing in the choir. It could help if you sing along with a more nervous applicant.

Reading the dots

Many singers in Gareth Malone-type choirs do not read music, at least not in the first instance. Some of them learn to do so through singing in the choir.

> 'I didn't join a choir for years because I thought you had to read music.'
>
> 'I couldn't read music at school so I thought there was no hope for me.'

If a significant number of your choir members cannot read music, it does not follow that you must plan for a unison choir. Given thought and preparation, it will be possible still to sing in harmony. Many choirs offer help to singers in learning to sing their 'parts'.

> 'I love it. I download my part and then I can listen to it on my way to work. I get some strange looks if I try singing along on the tube.'

A significant number of choir trainers have found it possible to record the parts separately, with them or another singer performing each part. Choir members then take home a pre-recorded CD in order to practise between rehearsals. In some choirs the recordings are made available in a members-only section of the choir website.

If you decide that reading music is essential to your choir, being clear about how you intend to help members to read music is important. All singers have different needs, and each one will probably perceive notation in a different way. One solution is to build into your training programme the option for some focused help for individuals who struggle with notation. Some more experienced readers could perhaps undertake an important mentoring role in the choir by working with those lacking in confidence in that area.

In some choirs, the process of reading music concentrates on the notes, perhaps even their letter names. In others, the emphasis is on following the shape of the melody or learning to recognise the sound and feel of the pitch intervals between the notes.

Rehearsals

If members of the choir are to retain their enthusiasm, rehearsals need to be on time, professional and enjoyable. If the practice is an hour long, it should last an hour. Of course, people want to catch up with each other, but it's much better to allow time and opportunity for this before or after the rehearsal.

There are lots of guides and resources for running a choir, but here are some basic points:

- Think about the time and place. If all your choir members are retired, is there any point in holding winter rehearsals after dark?
- Rehearsals in winter might not be best taking place in a cold church.
- Do all the choir members need to be present all the time?
- Could you take advantage of the experience and knowledge of some older members in order to give some one-to-one coaching to less-experienced members?

Warm-ups – no one would contemplate beginning a session at the gym without a warm-up, and it is just as essential before singing. They can be used creatively.

Some points related to warm-ups that could be worthy of consideration:

- What pitch is best for starting the first warm-up?
- What sort of dynamic is best for starting the first warm-up?
- Knowing what you hope to achieve, apart from pure warming up, is a good idea.
- Sharing that knowledge with the choir can give added purpose to the activity.
- What role does drawing the team of the choir together play in warm-ups?
- If you can devise warm-ups from tricky passages in the current repertoire you can achieve two objectives for the price of one.
- Is it possible to compose a warm-up based on awareness of a warm smooth tone, staccato, a particularly difficult interval, breath control in a long phrase?
- Is it possible to compose a warm-up based on a difficult passage for tuning, dynamics?

Rehearsals need to be challenging and encouraging. Sitting experienced members next to new members can be helpful. Often we stop the choir to tell them when something is wrong, but we may not be so ready to stop them to tell them about something they did well.

It is also important that individuals feel they are making progress. We owe it to them to find ways to make them aware of their own progress. We need to make sure that each member of the choir has a realistically achievable challenge.

Listening is vital not only for the choir trainer but also for each member of the choir. We need them to be able to spot issues of timing, tuning and balance for themselves. However bad you think your voice is, it is often better to demonstrate a passage by singing it rather than playing it on a piano. Developing a range of hand signals can be useful to avoid stopping in rehearsals and for making adjustments during performances.

It isn't always necessary to practise with the words. Without the words you can concentrate on pitch and tone, using vowels and consonants that project the sound forward. Reintroducing the words then brings them into focus. Do you tell the choir what difficult words and concepts mean? Do you ask the choir what difficult words and concepts mean?

On the whole, church choirs sing with music. Other types of choir often sing without music. It's good to try both. Most members will know a hymn or the text of an anthem from memory.

And take a break! When would it be useful in a rehearsal for the choir to stand? Why might it be useful for the choir to stand? Why might it be useful for the choir to sit? Do you allow for short breaks in the rehearsal, and what do you do during those in order to build choir confidence and identity?

Tact

Long-serving choir members who have developed a resistance to any thoughts of retirement, despite their voices being considerably less attractive than when they joined the choir, call for handling with extreme tact. Their service to the church is likely to have been admirable and will attract plaudits from members of the congregation who may well make judgements based on ethical rather than musical grounds.

Most choirs will harbour at least one difficult member. With age, the views of that member can become even more intransigent and, if they feel under threat or isolated, they are likely to become more vociferous. We wonder how many courses for choir trainers include a few practical sessions on tact. Positive approaches are more likely to bring about positive outcomes.

I belong to the choir

Everything is branded these days, but having a sense of identity and being proud to belong to an organisation create enthusiasm and loyalty. Names can be important and help to create a good image of the choir. A uniform can help, though it may also hinder. One of us remembers carefully discussing with the women of a church choir the wearing of black cloth caps. Most were in favour of getting rid of what they saw as very old-fashioned and unbecoming. They took a vote, and the overwhelming majority voted to abandon the headgear. The following Sunday the choir left their hats in the vestry, apart from two stalwart members who insisted on wearing them!

Whether or not the choir wear robes, what measures do you have in place to make sure they look as good as they sound?

Developing a sense of identity stems not only from the role the choir plays in the life of the church but also from the roles individual members play in the choir.

Questions for discussion

- What roles do you delegate to members of the choir?
- Have you a librarian?

- Have you a secretary?
- Have you a treasurer?
- Have you an attendance recorder?
- Does someone run a choir website? Is it part of the church website? Does it have a 'members only' section?
- Does the priest or minister have access to the 'members only' section?
- What do you include in that section, not only for information but to foster identity?
- Is the choir on Facebook? Might it be beneficial if they were?
- Might the task of running the website or Facebook page be a useful task to delegate to a member of the choir who has those skills, or to one who perhaps would like to learn those skills?

It is important in establishing the choir's identity that clergy promote a positive image of the choir in the church by thanking them in church services, referring to the music in sermons, attending choir practices occasionally, passing on comments from the congregation, encouraging them to participate in other church events, inviting them to organise a stall at the annual bazaar, and so on.

Youth and adult choirs

The traditional cathedral choir consisted of men and boys, and this model was followed in larger parish churches. In small churches women and men were joined by a few youngsters. Undoubtedly it is good for people of different ages to share in joint activities, and children and young people can be every bit as musical and wise as adults – if not more so. However, people learn in different ways, and children and adults may have different educational needs. Nowadays girls grace cathedral choir stalls, which may see a range of choirs. All churches can benefit from a variety of musical groups as long as there is a clear role identified for each and full collaboration between all the musicians.

Some choirs have looked towards building for the future with a youth choir. It is tempting to hope that recruiting children will lead to such an outcome in a few years' time. To maintain the interest of 8-year-olds and 15-year-olds in the same group represents a challenge.

Many schools find it difficult or impossible to recruit teachers with some musical knowledge and experience. That means that it is quite likely that there is a school in your area which is struggling to find somebody to run a lunchtime singing group. That somebody could be you, and the singing group could prove to be useful in finding new singers for a church youth choir.

Clergy and choir

> 'I would not be happy to have the minister at choir practice.'
>
> 'We would welcome her to join us on practice nights and have invited her to attend, but she seems wary of joining us.'

Some clergy benefit from regarding the choir as a pastoral catalyst. Many have found that it is possible to use the choir to reach out into the community. With which elements of pastoral support can the choir assist?

Some clergy find it useful to attend choir practices in order to understand the choir 'from the inside', while sadly others find their presence is resented. In such cases it might be useful to agree what role the priest or minister will play in choir practices. In some cases they might like to sing. They might be invited to give a context to the words of a hymn or anthem. Some clergy like to make encouraging comments to the choir. Most choirs appreciate such comments.

Concerts

> 'Our organist draws on her musical contacts to provide musicians for concerts.'
>
> 'I love the different music we can learn when we are working for a concert.'
>
> 'I don't know about it being a church choir. It is really much more of a community choir.'

One way of bringing the choir to the church and community's attention is through concerts and other performances outside church services. This may also enable the choir to vary their repertoire. In addition, it may offer an opportunity for members of the choir to sing solos or perform on an instrument. Performing at the harvest supper or a church social event, singing madrigals on a summer evening or participating in a local community will inspire confidence and enthusiasm.

Joining with other musicians for a concert can also broaden the musical horizons of the choir and therefore of the community. A choirmaster tells of a chance encounter with a car salesman who played steel pans. He reports that joining together with the pans for a concert really energised the choir.

What can you give?

A church choir is an amazing resource, and there are many churches that could be helped by those who have one. Help could be given in starting up a new choir, perhaps by first contributing to a church service.

Music is expensive and often needs to be arranged to suit the make-up of the choir. Offers to lend or arrange music would be gratefully received by many churches.

Clergy will probably know from their colleagues the needs of neighbouring churches and could help in bringing choirs together for mutual support and help.

It may be that you can offer help to another church that would like to start a choir. It is important to know what sort of help and advice you can offer. How can you make your help practical rather than theoretical? How can your choir offer help to another church that wants to start a choir?

A benefice choir

Within the local area, there are possibilities of producing a choir consisting of members of several different churches, or a number of choirs could join together for special services or a concert.

Finding the resources

> 'It is challenging to maintain a choir and resources, robes, music, etc.'
>
> 'I run a supporters club for the choir. We not only raise funds but we also try to help in practical ways like arranging some babysitting for a young couple who sing in the choir.'

In many churches the cost of musicians is more than available finance can support, but many choirs thrive even in those conditions. In some of those an independent choir fund is the lifesaver.

If that sounds like a good idea, start to work on a strategy for launching the idea in your church.

> If a choir fund might be valuable in your church, here are some points for consideration and discussion:
>
> - Who might you particularly target in order to launch the fund?
> - Would it help if you made explicit what you hope to spend the money on?
> - It might not just be a case of purchasing music. What other funds will be needed for the type of choir at your church?

Sadly, too often we have tripped over a pile of unused music in one church that might be very useful to a church in the next village. It might be worthwhile setting up a dialogue with other churches in order to share resources, even if you do all need the harvest anthem on the same Sunday.

We've mentioned the importance for choir members of knowing about their role in the choir. If you have a choir fund:

- might a choir member run it?
- might a choir member take responsibility for purchasing new music?
- might a choir member take responsibility for making sure that the robes, etc. are all in good order?

Some choirs are maintained by a choir supporters club. This is often most effective where the choir has a public role within the community. The supporters club raises funds by organising social and other events for the benefit of the community. The choir may underline its identity further by performing at some of those events.

> If a supporters club might be valuable in your church, here are some points for consideration and discussion:
>
> - Who might you target within your community to join the supporters club?
> - What would they get out of belonging?
> - Could a choir member run the supporters club?
> - How could your priest or minister help by using their knowledge of the community and of individuals within the community?
> - Would it be possible for the choir to offer some benefits to members of the supporters club?

Happy singing.

SEVEN

Where have all the organists gone?

> 'We have no organist for our weekly service. There is just nobody in sight.'
>
> 'Our small band of organists play because they want to contribute to village life.'
>
> 'We took part in a scheme locally where an experienced organist gave a short series of lessons to some interested pianists.'
>
> 'I need to find someone to help me improve what I can do on the organ.'
>
> 'Our organist is in his nineties but plays wonderfully. Our challenge is to find someone to follow in his footsteps.'
>
> 'Our organist is good but quite old.'
>
> 'Our organist died three years ago and has not been replaced.'
>
> 'We would struggle if our current organist resigned.'

It is not unusual for clergy to discover that finding an organist to play on a regular basis is very difficult – indeed, it can be impossible. Gone are the days when an advertisement would bring two or three replies and interviews could follow. In some places, knowledge of the position of middle C might well rank as a vital qualification.

A quick survey of the heads of churchgoers reveals that grey is the predominant hair colour in many places, and the increasing average age of many congregations finds a parallel with the average age of organists. The limited success in recruiting young people to many congregations is mirrored in the lack of success in recruiting young organists. Worship bands often offer an opportunity for students to play their flute, violin or guitar, but then the students reach university age and leave home and church in order to study. Constant re-recruitment is therefore necessary, and those who lead worship bands can find themselves rebuilding the group every three or four years.

> 'With the high levels of engineering in much of today's music it is impossible for worship groups to sound anything but very amateur.'

We expect a high level of performance and production from professional groups, and this expectation is often reflected in what we expect from a worship band. Students playing flute, guitar and violin together with a cheap electric keyboard will not achieve that. This mismatch of sound expectation is a problem peculiar to worship bands. Most members of a congregation may not expect the organ to sound as though it is being played by an internationally acclaimed artist, whereas expectations of bands can be a different matter.

Whatever musicians you aim to recruit, knowledge of the community is vital. While writing this book we met several clergy who had no idea that an underemployed organist was living in their parish. Noting musical ability in parishioners does not appear to be a hobby greatly practised by clergy, but it is one that is becoming imperative, since converting pianists to a level of competency at which they could be valuable as church musicians is the only way forward.

'Closing the sale' seems to mark another point of reticence.

> 'I don't like to feel that I am imposing on a well-intentioned parishioner.'
>
> 'It is embarrassing to ask.'

That is a pity, because learning to adapt skills, even those of some long standing, can be a richly rewarding experience. And if you don't ask, you will deny the potential candidate that opportunity.

> 'I've really enjoyed getting to grips with the organ and I feel that I am doing something to keep alive a tradition in the village. I didn't think I would be able to do that.'

Clergy should be reassured that they are not on their own in the search. Local musical groups and associations of organists may be able to help, as may some schools. Some churches have discovered a rich vein of musicians, many of them pianists, about to move to university in a year or so and who are therefore in the sixth form. Some basic tuition in organ playing has enabled the students to add another 'qualification' to their CV and simultaneously enriched their university application.

Using members of the congregation as a search party will help them to feel useful and widen the spread of the net.

It is possible that your diocese or district runs a young organists scheme. If they don't, perhaps you could try to persuade them that it would be worthwhile.

Questions for discussion

- What benefits might follow from asking members of the congregation to help you to find someone to play in church?

- What might be the pitfalls?
- What benefits might follow from asking local schools for help?
- Have you asked your local organists' association for help?
- Have you made enquiries with any local music groups?
- Does your denomination run any music committees at a district, regional or diocesan level?

Playing the piano and playing the organ are two different things. If you are successful in finding a willing candidate, you have a responsibility to them to seek out someone to give basic tuition in hymn and service playing. The place to start might well be at the nearest church that has an organist with a reasonable level of competence.

> 'We have a regular young organist. We need to find some mentoring and training for him.'
>
> 'I was surprised when the church at the other end of the town asked if I could give some lessons to a pianist who thought they might be able to pick up the organ. I'm even more surprised to say I have enjoyed doing it, even though, at first, I didn't think I would be the best person.'

Supporting a potential organist

Some pianists of experience are loath to accept lessons and may feel more comfortable trying to adapt their piano skills by themselves.

> 'I am a pianist and I know that I don't play the organ like an organ.'
>
> 'I wouldn't mind having a go by myself. Perhaps I would not get very far but I could try it out.'

In the appendix we have written some notes to help pianists wanting to learn a few basics about organ-playing technique. These notes can be photocopied.

> 'I'm embarrassed to admit to being an organist. People think it is stuffy and irrelevant.'

Many church musicians do not have a very high self-esteem. Some have found that helping young musicians to gain a familiarity and basic skill at the organ has a positive effect on their own self-image, as well as securing a future for the role of the organ in their church.

Before you set up your own local conversion course for pianists, it would be advisable to invest in some security checks on those who are going to be working with the students, particularly if they are under 18. Ensure that all involved are aware of your church's child protection policy.

> 'I know my days are numbered. I can't play as well as I used to. The minister suggested I might be able to help a lady who plays the piano. I surprised myself really because I found I could.'

Faced with an elderly organist who is gradually becoming less able to play as well as they would like, it will be necessary to adopt a gentle and sympathetic approach. An elderly organist might be useful in mentoring a young potential organist. They might well take a pride in passing on their experience, knowledge and skills, while helping to provide a solution to the skills shortage.

> 'We are very lucky to have a brilliant organist.'
>
> 'We have three people who can play the organ.'
>
> 'Our organist is fine but we have a shortage of deputies.'
>
> 'Finding organists for weddings and funerals is a real problem.'
>
> 'I am one of two volunteer organists who alternate most Sundays.'
>
> 'I wish other organists would be willing to help out in more than one church as I do.'
>
> 'Our young volunteer organist is gaining in confidence and can gradually do more and more.'

So finding organists is not impossible. Many churches operate a rota system with a group of organists, booking some months in advance. This has advantages in so far that it is usually possible to cover holidays. It also offers the congregation the opportunity to enjoy several different styles of accompaniment, and some will prefer one to another. Rotas do not work so well with choir leaders, where the presence of a regular musician each week is more vital.

Payment

> 'We have only one organist for the whole group of churches. She is overworked and not paid.'
>
> 'We cannot afford to pay a musician.'

The differences in the rates of remuneration paid by churches for Sunday services, and in the rates churches pass on from the public in terms of remuneration for weddings and funerals, is often marked. In fact, despite all the usual justifications, it does not bear close investigation. A doubling of the wedding rate when the service is recorded has promoted press comment in recent years.

Before deciding on any rates of pay, it is good for the church community to think about those who are paid for their services within the church. Many people, from wardens and stewards to treasurers, church cleaners and magazine editors, offer their time and abilities as part of their Christian giving. A congregation may have qualified electricians and builders, for example, who will offer their skills in the service of the church. There is no reason why church musicians should not do the same. Equally, if the church has a need and there are no volunteers within the congregation or known to the church, there is every justification for paying for professional services.

In the Orthodox tradition, nearly all the service is sung. The liturgy partly consists of a dialogue between the clergy and the choir. The prayers are chanted following a prescribed musical form, and almost nothing is read in a normal speaking voice, with the exception of the homily if one is given. Because the human voice is seen as the most perfect instrument of praise, musical instruments are not generally used to accompany the choir. If the worship is to be truly uplifting and inspiring within such a tradition, it is vital that a small group of competent singers is employed.

Money often focuses our minds and can promote a worthwhile discussion about the musical needs of the church and the price the church is willing to pay to fulfil those needs. Whether the work is paid for or done voluntarily, expectations should be clear, and the highest standards sought.

EIGHT

When it goes wrong

We have seen plenty of examples of things going wrong or events being on the cusp of disaster. This chapter, like the others, is written for both clergy and musicians. Sadly, both can make mistakes and behave unwisely. Whatever sparks the crisis, the real problem will usually be more deeply rooted and will have built up over a period of time. It makes sense to try to deal with the deep-rooted problem before it grows even stronger roots.

> 'Well, he was new to the job and first he didn't like the tunes I suggested for several weeks, then he didn't like a piece of music that I played, and I thought I knew where we were heading so I asked to have a chat.'

Faced with 'a chat', this organist will probably open with the immediate problem rather than introducing the underlying problem, which is his unease that his priest or minister does not seem to have much respect for his musical judgement. How, and on which level, will his minister respond? The choice of tunes for hymns and the choice of music performed is a matter for personal judgement. The minister may have a point. So may the organist. They may be able to find some common ground, especially if they can understand each other's point of view. But if the minister really does not respect the organist's musical judgement, there will not be much air to clear, and a deterioration in the relationship may well be inevitable.

However, the minister would do well to remind himself that he is new to the job and perhaps acting hastily. Asking elders, wardens and members of the congregation for their opinions would help him to discover how much support there is for the organist.

If the minister does not realise his own insensitivity, there is a more difficult challenge, involving an openness to acknowledge the offence caused and a willingness from both parties to get on with life. Both parties may feel a need to agree about methods of working in the future, but if such arrangements are not the result of a deep-seated problem, they may be more trouble and make more work. Both parties must recognise that problems can arise as a result of human fallibility. Who is not guilty of being thoughtless, forgetful or clumsy in some way at some time?

Without the 'chat', the problem is more likely to fester and lead to an atmosphere of mistrust which will deepen on both sides. This may well manifest itself as an increasingly difficult breakdown in relationships.

> 'She seems to be over-sensitive. After all, I am only human and I admit I make mistakes. Well, at least I learned that I have to be more careful in future.'
>
> 'I was so furious and stormed in to sort it out and made such a fool of myself.'

Trying to sort anything out while you are in a temper is unlikely to bring a positive outcome.

> 'It was like being called to the head teacher's study.'

In any discussion there will be three elements in play: the spoken word, the tone in which they are spoken and the body language. Those are listed in reverse order of the impact they will make. The real key might be for both parties to take note of what was not said. Perhaps the body language in the example above was not altogether helpful.

Showing respect and searching for understanding are often more important than agreeing.

Questions for discussion

- Can you focus on the meaning rather than getting caught up in the words?
- Can you stay open-minded and avoid making assumptions or judgements?
- Do you believe that the other person will listen to you only if you will listen to them?

Sharing a problem with a colleague or writing about the problem in a document addressed only to you might help. It is always worth wondering whether the behaviour of another is caused by an underlying issue with which they have to deal. Few musicians or clergy live charmed, trouble-free lives.

Complaints are gregarious. If one person makes a complaint against another, the other will often react by making a complaint against the initiator. There may be two levels of response, apart from avoidance. Conciliation implies discussion, which may lead to a positive outcome. It only works if both parties want it to work. Confrontation is the last resort, and is less likely to lead to a happy outcome.

The attitudes of both parties may be fundamental to a problem. If you are brave enough, you could learn a great deal by examining where your attitude is based. Most attitudes are based in a personal opinion and beliefs that are reinforced by a peer group. It probably goes without saying that trying to see the other person's point of view is going to be more helpful than guarding your own. One important decision to reach is whether it is possible to draw a line under past differences and move on.

Mediation may help, provided the mediator remains neutral. This may not be easy if the mediator has an existing relationship with one or both of the offended parties. A good mediator can help both parties to articulate their view, clarify the difficulties, help the parties to find options that address the issues and document any agreements reached. A trained and experienced mediator may be able to go further in helping the parties to express and understand each other's feelings and experiences, and encouraging them to take responsibility for their contribution to the past, and assist in healing the relationship.

Arbitration is a more serious step, in which both parties make their grievance clear and agree to accept the decision of a third party.

If a serious complaint is made about you it would be wise to seek legal advice at an early stage.

The extreme option open to an organist is resignation. This is a serious step and should be preceded by careful thought. Are the difficulties with the priest/minister common to other church officers? Is there a breakdown in relations with the choir or officers of the church? Coming to the decision that in staying one is doing more harm than good is not an easy exercise in soul-searching.

Leaving can be a traumatic experience for an organist. You will have built a relationship with many members of the choir and congregation. You will certainly have built a relationship with the organ, the foibles of which you will know and understand as no other. Leaving with dignity is even more difficult. Who can make a bald statement that 'while wishing everybody well, I think that it is time to move on'? It is certainly not easy.

Musicians may wish to note that all denominations have their own procedures for disciplining their ministers.

Contracts

In the UK there are no standard expectations regarding duties, qualifications or payments to church musicians. Every church will consider what might be appropriate given their individual circumstances. A contract can be valuable as a way of setting out clear expectations of both the musician and the church authorities.

Even if a formal contract is not considered appropriate, some form of working agreement could be helpful. Care is needed with such informal arrangements. One person's understanding of a sentence or paragraph can be very different from that of another. When disputes arise, both parties can sometimes be found brandishing the same piece of paper and claiming their own unique point of view.

Questions for discussion

- What are your expectations for a musician in terms of time and responsibility?
- Will you be able to reflect the qualifications and experience of the musician?
- What are the resources of your church?

If the musician is to have responsibility for recruitment, preparation of repertoire, administration and pastoral care, especially where young people are involved, this must be reflected in the remuneration, which would be more generous than that offered to a musician whose responsibility is restricted to accompanying a service. Qualifications are fine things, but so is experience, and many organists will not have both.

Some musicians may be willing to work without remuneration. In the event of a change of regime the cost of a replacement can be a shock to the treasurer. It is important that a church musician feels valued. Even a musician who offers their service free of charge may appreciate some token of respect and thanks for the hours of dedicated preparation and practice that have led to effective accompaniment of the services.

Advice on paying church musicians is available from the Royal School of Church Music.[12] A specimen contract is also available to download, whether you are a member or not, from the RSCM. The advice section of the Incorporated Society of Musicians website gives advice on how to calculate organists' fees.[13]

A contract is a legally binding agreement between two or more people. Each party to a contract is bound by what the contract says. If anyone departs from the contract, they could be liable to the other parties.

In English law a contract does not have to be written, so in practice, any musician who contributes to the music in a church probably has a form of contract. Written contracts can be useful to clarify what the church and the organist can expect from one another, and to provide a safety valve in the event of something going wrong. That way, at least a minimum level of cooperation is ensured.

After setting out terms and definitions, most contracts should cover:

- the scope of the post;
- responsibility of extra services;
- responsibility for weddings and funerals;
- payments;

12. Royal School of Church Music. Available at http://www.rscm.com/music-and-resources/advice-and-information/paying-church-musicians/ (accessed 4 May 2016).
13. Incorporated Society of Musicians. Available at http://www.ism.org/advice/employed-organist-fees (accessed 19 April 2016).

- holidays;
- sickness, including arrangements for maternity and paternity;
- use of the organ;
- any pension arrangements;
- trade union arrangements;
- agreed arrangements for cooperation, grievance and discipline;
- agreements regarding termination of the contract.

S. S. Wesley's magnificent anthem, 'Blessed be the God and Father', contains the moving line 'See that ye love one another'; musicians and clergy might well benefit from taking that exhortation seriously.

'A friend of mine took it seriously and married the vicar.'

NINE

Instruments and maintenance

The instruments used for worship in your church may be many and various. In most churches, only the larger instruments are likely to be the property of the church.

Organs

> 'I love the organ, especially when it is being played quietly. Even then it is still a big sound.'
>
> 'The sound pictures of the organ are all-important.'

To many, the sound of a pipe organ is what church music is all about. All the same, pipe organs take up a fairly unreasonable amount of room in a church – at least, so we are told from time to time. They are also costly to maintain. As they grow older they are likely to become increasingly unreliable, and when organs go wrong they often do it fairly loudly. A note stuck on in the middle of a service can soon become more than embarrassing.

> 'Our biggest difficulty is the cost of maintaining a pipe organ.'
>
> 'The church is unlikely ever to be able to restore the organ.'
>
> 'Expensive work is long overdue on the organ.'
>
> 'I don't even know if the organ still works. Nobody has played it for years.'

The organ may well be redundant in a church that has moved on towards a different kind of music in worship. It might well then take very little time for a suggestion to emerge that the organ be scrapped as the space would be just right for something else. In some cases the decision may be taken to purchase an electronic organ.

> 'Just keeping the pipe organ going was costing much too much so we decided to purchase an electronic organ. We were shocked to find that we almost could not give the pipe organ away.'

You may well find that the pipe organ which has graced your church for many years and has cost a fortune to maintain is of little – if any – cash value.

A pipe organ that has been well maintained can still be giving reliable service a hundred years after it was installed, although it will probably have needed significant attention three or four times during that century of service. The pipes themselves are likely to last indefinitely, although some may sag with age. The action work of a pipe organ is more likely to become problematic.

An electronic organ may come with an attractive ten-year guarantee. It might still be working in 25 years' time, but the technology upon which it is based will, in that period of time, have developed hugely. If anything goes wrong, parts may be difficult to obtain 25 years on. Damp churches do not engender longevity in electronic equipment. Electronic instruments built 25 years ago often sound very basic and dated today. Technology has advanced so far and so quickly, and will probably continue to do so.

> 'As a boy I visited a church every year on holiday and they let me use the little two-manual pipe organ for practice. One summer I was shocked to find that the organ had been disposed of and a large four-manual electronic organ had replaced it. The organist was euphoric about the new instrument but they would not let me use it for practice. It lasted about 20 years, perhaps not even so long before they had to get rid of it as it was impossible to repair.'

However, an electronic instrument will take up far less room than the pipe equivalent, and cost far less. It will not need tuning and should only need occasional maintenance. It will also offer a wider range of sounds than a small pipe organ. Organists used to amuse themselves by sharing the thought that although an electronic organ could offer a larger range of sounds, all those sounds sounded the same. This is not even remotely true today. Those who advise that a single manual pipe organ is all that is required for a church seating 150 may be well advised to use the word 'required'. It might be a limited generator of fun, though.

Electronic organs can raise controversy very easily. A respected colleague who builds pipe organs was recently incensed at the notion that he might like to attend a session at which several of us hoped to find out more about the potential of electronic organs.

> 'I'd rather play a good quality electronic organ than a poor quality pipe organ.'

Faced with playing a service on a badly maintained pipe organ that has developed an eccentric character and is difficult to control, many organists would probably choose the electronic alternative. An electronic instrument can sound very impressive if supplied with decent speakers. The quality of the speakers is fundamental to obtaining an impressive sound in a building of church proportions, and an electronic organ can also be comfortable to play and easy to control.

It is possible to add to your electronic instrument sampled stops from organs around the world. By connecting your electronic organ to a computer, a library of sounds will be available to you to use in services and recitals. You can perform on historic instruments and call up sounds that might best suit the style of the music you are performing, whether baroque, classical or symphonic. You can even call up the sounds of theatre and cinema organs.

All the same, not all organists will agree on the merits of electronic instruments. At the point when you need to advertise for a new organist, you will therefore expect to receive a shorter list of applicants.

Many electronic instruments are imported to this country, having been built in the Netherlands or Italy. By arrangement, you can visit the showrooms of the suppliers in this country and try many of the models available. Even better, it is often possible for the supplier to bring an organ to your church so that you can see and hear what it sounds like in your building. Many suppliers will even be happy to leave the instrument with you for a period of time so that you can use it in services and obtain opinions from the choir and congregation. When you have been flooded with views, you may well be even more confused.

We have underlined the importance of high-quality speakers, but finding the best site for those speakers is also vital. Some churches hide the speakers behind the front pipes of the pipe organ case. This allows the remainder of the pipe organ to be removed, making space available for other use. Try listening to the electronic organ through good quality headphones and compare what you hear with what you hear from the speakers. If the headphones win noticeably, look again at the quality of the speakers.

Replacing a tired pipe organ with a new pipe organ is relatively rare, probably because of the cost of doing so. During the second half of the twentieth century many unfashionable pipe organs were destroyed in favour of new installations in a scramble to obtain 'authentic' (whatever that means) baroque sounds. Many fine instruments were lost as a consequence, and numerous churches were left with instruments that make a fair sound in the baroque repertoire but struggle to impress in other styles.

> 'I wonder at organs such as this one. Look – two eight-foot stops and two four-foot stops and the rest just screech at you. Fifty years ago they probably thought that was better than the lovely old Hill organ that stood here.'

Much consideration should be given before a decision is made to scrap any existing organ. Does the organ that you are about to scrap represent fine work? Is it of historical significance? Is it one of very few left by the particular builder? It was probably designed for the acoustic in your particular building and may well, when it is working, produce the most beautiful sounds. On the other hand, there are a fair number of organs in buildings to which they are unsuited. Perhaps they make an ungrateful sound: perhaps coarse, edgy and vulgar; perhaps timid and insufficient to lead singing in the building. Help is at hand: a short survey of the internet will produce results for a whole range of organ advisers, and advisers to your own denomination will be able to furnish assistance as well.

It is possible that a congregation that decided 20 years previously to scrap their pipe organ can now find themselves in a position to undertake the necessary work on that organ. There could be merit in mothballing an organ that is ceasing to give service and replacing it for the time being with an electronic instrument. Who knows what the future will hold? We have seen several congregations learn to love their pipe organ once again, even though service music is provided by an excellent worship band.

> 'A group of us started to wonder what that thing actually did and if it was any good, so we contacted the county organists' association and they took a look and we found we had an unexpected treasure sitting there not being used. We don't need it in our worship but we are currently exploring ways in which we can use it to the benefit of our community.'

> 'We've got this instrument. Nobody knows much about it. How are we going to use it?'

It follows that, if it is difficult to give some organs away, it must be possible to purchase a second-hand organ fairly cheaply – and that is indeed the case. Before you rush to do so, though, spend some time obtaining quotations for the cost of removal from the present site and installation in your church. It will not be cheap, but you could provide a fine instrument for your church and give a new lease of life to a set of pipes. Local organ builders and advisers often know of redundant organs, and there are lists available on the internet. It may not seem highly attractive to obtain an organ that has already given more than 150 years of service, but the quality of workmanship in a well-made Victorian organ is likely to give many more years, especially when compared with some organs of a later date.

> 'We decided that, with limited cash, we only had one option, and that was to build our own organ. We did not realise how much work was involved.'

> 'I don't think we would ever do it again. We started with a team of volunteers who all had useful skills. Sadly some of those are no longer with us. There was great enthusiasm when we were removing the organ from the previous church and I admit it was great fun. Even the early days of erection in our church were positive and the main bits took shape fairly quickly. We told ourselves that it would be done by Christmas but it has taken years and it is still not really finished or reliable.'
>
> 'I'd say don't go down the DIY route. We are left having to pay an organ builder to finish the job and he is having to remove much of the work that we did because it was not reliable. It is a nightmare.'
>
> 'The organist was the only person who really understood it and he left. We are in a mess.'

Beware of taking on the job of installation as a DIY project. It will be tempting and you could save the church thousands of pounds, but pipe organs are often more complicated than they appear, and a well-used instrument will need some replacement of parts. It is very rare for an organ to fit exactly into a new building. Even so, the job of dismantling and putting it all together again will, although fascinating, not be easy. When adaptations have to be made to suit the new site, these are best left to professionals. At the end of a DIY project you will also have no guarantee of the quality or assurance of attention for the future.

Pipe organs need tuning regularly. Some of the finest in the land are tuned on a monthly basis. Few churches can afford that level of maintenance. Use a qualified tuner. Most will offer a tuning contract. Tuning visits are often arranged for the autumn, after the heating has been switched on, and for the spring, often in preparation for Easter, when the heating has been, probably prematurely, retired. On many organs the flue pipes will stand in tune fairly reliably and may not need tuning. The reed pipes will often be more of a problem. As temperature and humidity vary, the reeds and flues will move out of tune with each other. It might be as well to have the reeds tuned more frequently than the whole organ.

Most organ tuners will carry out small repairs as part of a tuning visit, but it is not equitable to rely on their good nature to undertake more than minor work at such a visit. A pipe organ will reach a stage where it will need overhaul and general repair. It is wise to listen to the advice of the organist who will know when the organ is beginning to give signs of serious trouble. When an overhaul is planned it may also be an appropriate time to make improvements to the organ, perhaps in the form of some tonal alterations (changes to the stops and pipework).

In such instances it would be well to bear in mind the following:

- Reports and quotations should be obtained from several organ builders.
- An independent organ adviser should be involved.
- Where the existing organ is in a poor state, it may be best to replace it with a new or second-hand instrument.
- Any relocation of an organ or alteration to the specification or action requires careful consideration. The original design for an organ aims to present an artistic unity. Adding new stops or modifying existing stops, however desirable it might appear, will almost always destroy that unity of artistic purpose. There may also be specific bodies that need to be involved, especially if the organ has historical interest.
- Grants, sometimes quite generous, can be sought for the restoration of a historic organ.
- Depending on the denomination, permissions will need to be obtained.

Organ blowers must be the most neglected part of an instrument until they give up the ghost. We have had that experience twice. It may surprise you to know that your organ tuner possibly pays no attention to the blower on tuning visits and that you need to find specialist assistance with maintenance.

Pipe organs are affected by both damp and dryness. Serious and costly cracks in the woodwork can result from over-enthusiastic use of heating.

It is possible to insure organs. Consideration of insurance is complex, however. If the organ were damaged by fire or vandalism, would it be rebuilt? Would the heritage value of the instrument be lost in those circumstances? What would replace an organ that was destroyed? What would replace an organ that was partly destroyed?

If your church is to be redecorated or building work is to be undertaken, it is essential that the organ is covered and protected, under supervision of the organ builder. This may put it out of action for the duration of the work, and taking off the covers needs supervision as well.

Pianos

Many churches possess pianos in varying degrees of reliability, and many of the comments set out previously with regard to aged organs might also apply to church pianos. If an instrument is to give aesthetic pleasure it should be capable, at least, of standing in tune. And if it is capable, it should be tuned regularly. Once a piano loses pitch it is a major operation to return it to pitch. Church buildings are no more friendly towards pianos than they are to organs. If a grand piano is to be moved around the building, inevitably over uneven floors, it is important that the legs are strengthened with a metal frame or its travelling days will be short-lived.

> 'We use an electric piano because we have somebody to play it.'

Particularly when a worship band is involved, churches often purchase an electronic piano. Well, we wish they would. Too often they purchase an electronic keyboard that is not touch-sensitive and does not make attractive sounds, but does play a large library of what are termed 'rhythms'. Quite often they rely on the services of the student who is going to play the instrument to bring their own from home.

In a church acoustic, a good quality electronic piano can sound impressive. It is also capable of creating a vast range of sounds that can be used very effectively with a worship group. Some of the arguments for and against electronic organs will also apply.

Electronic pianos, like their acoustic counterparts, can be heavy to move around. They usually demand lifting. Whether the piano is acoustic or electronic, it is well worth purchasing a good-quality cover for it and dissuading the flower arrangers from leaving displays on top of the instrument.

Concluding voluntary

> 'In the parish, people turn up to have a good sing, to meet their neighbours, and to enjoy a cup of lukewarm instant coffee, just like always. For their music, some put their trust in Marbeck, and some in drum kits. Some do both.'[14]

We have written this book out of a conviction that music can bring life and energy to worship. It can not only lift our spirits but also attract others to become involved in our faith. Music has played a major part in all revivals of Christian communities, and as the church seeks to renew itself and face the challenges of the twenty-first century, the role of music is as vital as ever.

In our research for this book, we have become even more aware of the thousands of volunteers who, week by week, are involved in the music-making of their churches. At a time when the Church is changing and when many outside it are sceptical about its place in society, their contribution needs to be valued and nurtured all the more.

We believe that music, like the Holy Spirit, pervades our whole world, thrills us, moves us, binds us together and speaks to us across barriers of language. If music is important to the Church's mission and ministry, the whole church community must support its musical leaders and be involved in decisions to do with their work. Church councils, elders, etc. must embrace the responsibility for harnessing the musical gifts and sensitivities in all of us into the process of creating the music style for their church community.

What keeps us motivated as musicians is the sparkle of creation and imagination that we discover in music and the joy of collaborating with other musicians. In our talks with people in churches where music is thriving, we have been struck by the creativity, imagination and collaboration they bring to their worship. Churches where ministers, musicians, readers, intercessors and members of the congregation regularly sit down and discuss their church's worship are alive with ideas. Of course, the busy pace of working lives means that sometimes we have to slot musical contributions into set patterns of liturgy. Yet where all who are responsible for worship are able to contribute and pool ideas and resources, the Spirit leads us to a deeper awareness of God's presence.

We have seen the Spirit at work not only in the collaboration of ministry and worship teams, but also outside the church. In our communities we have rejoiced in the exuberance of community choirs, in the dedication of youngsters learning instruments, and in the way

14. Andrew Gant, *O Sing unto the Lord*, p.372.

music is so accessible and pervades all our lives. All this needs to be embraced by the Church. While being confident of our own unique contribution to the world of music, we need to be bold in exploring and learning from all that contemporary music-making offers.

The text that has come back to us again and again in our experience of collaborating on this guide is from John's Gospel: 'God is spirit, and those who worship him must worship in spirit and truth' (John 4:24).

Appendix

You are welcome to photocopy this appendix, as long as the source is acknowledged.

Perhaps you are able to play the piano and would like to translate those skills and learn a few basics about playing an organ. Help and guidance from an organist is highly desirable. If you feel that such help is not available, these notes may offer you a suggested pathway along which to take your first steps.

Adapting to an organ

First you will have to pull out a stop or two. Try those with 8′ on them.

If you try to play part of a piece that you are familiar with from the piano, the most obvious difference between playing a piano and playing an organ will instantly become clear. Once you release a note on an organ, the sound is gone. There is also no sustaining pedal. Try playing as though your fingers are stuck to the keys. Imagine that you have glue on your fingers.

The next difference is the need to set up sounds using the stops.

> 'I pull out this one and this one and this one and that does me perfectly well for the whole service.'

Most will want to be a little more adventurous and reflect the mood of the service by their choice of stops. Trying different sounds and finding ones that you like is the best way. Hold down a chord and try every stop on that manual (keyboard). Some will be quieter or louder; others will be higher or lower.

If you think that the 8ft stops work at piano pitch, you are right. The 4ft stops make the sounds an octave higher. The 2ft stops make the sounds two octaves higher, and 16ft stops sound an octave lower than piano pitch.

By adding a 4ft stop to an 8ft stop you brighten the tone.

By adding a 2ft stop to the above you brighten it still more.

By adding a 16ft stop to an 8ft stop you give weight to the tone.

There may be some pedals or little buttons (called pistons) under the keyboards.

> 'I just press that thing and away we go.'

These bring out groups of stops and could provide useful groups for loud verses and quieter verses. As well as using these, try using some stops by hand, as this will add to the character of the sounds you make. Try playing verses of hymns with glue-covered fingers and using different combinations of stops. If you set different stops on the two (or more) manuals, you can add a variety of sounds to your playing by moving from one to the other.

The pedal keyboard

Some pianists will reach this far without too much trouble, but the pedal keyboard is nearly always a stumbling block. Few pianists with some technical ability relish the idea of returning to square one with their hands in order to incorporate a pedal technique.

> 'I don't touch those.'
>
> 'I just put in the pedal note for the end of each line of the hymn.'
>
> 'We have built a removable cover that goes over the pedals to make it more comfortable for the lady who plays.'

Don't give up on the pedals! For most it has to begin with pedal-only exercises. Most pianists don't mind those too much. They can also enjoy finding their way around the pedal keyboard using the gaps between the 'black notes' and realising that the layout of the notes is similar to a piano keyboard. You may also find pedal markings for the use of the heel (a small circle) and for the toe (an arrow head). Markings above the note imply use of the right foot and a mark under the note denotes a role for the left foot.

A next stage might be to take a very simple hymn and try just playing over the left-hand part. Then do it again, very slowly, and add the bass part on the pedal keyboard. Many pianists find this very difficult, so it really does need to be slow before you try to increase the tempo gradually. Start with just a couple of chords. You will need to spend hours practising this in order to make some progress, and many organists will by now be holding up their hands in horror and telling you that the bass part should be played using the pedal keyboard while the tenor part is played with the left hand. They are right, but in hymns it might not matter too much.

You've guessed that the next step might be to add your right hand. You will also have guessed that the advice is to take it slowly.

There are collections of pieces arranged for manuals only. Indeed, many of the pieces you play on the piano, especially the baroque ones, will work well on the organ once you have become used to the difference in touch. You will find that you may have to change the fingering in order to achieve the smooth flow of notes on the organ.

'I've decided to forget about the pedal notes at first. I'll come back to them when I've got more confidence.'

Beware. Few who walk down this path ever manage to come back. There is a natural disinclination to spend hours in a cold church trying to come to grips with the pedal keyboard. Overcome it.

Improvisation

Without falling into the trap of trying to fill every silence in the service, improvisation is a skill needed by all who play for services. Yet many potential organists will be hesitant to even try.

'I don't do improvisation.'

'I get by somehow but I couldn't show you how.'

'I don't understand how you can know what notes to play.'

'I wouldn't know where to begin.'

The quotations above come from regular service organists.

Our first advice would be to find some help from a teacher. That may not be easy, as many who are willing to teach the organ are unwilling to teach improvisation.

For those who would like to know where to begin, we offer some examples of possible methods for improvisation on hymn tunes.

For a gentle improvisation

- Choose a tune with four lines.
- Choose a gentle flute sound on the swell for your left hand and a flute on the great for your right hand, or play both hands on the swell. Perhaps couple the swell to the great. You will find a stop called Swell to Great. It will do that for you.
- Play the first line with melody only.
- Play the second line with thirds below the melody. You can use both hands to do this. If you are not sure, a third is the next-but-one note.
- Play the third line with thirds and fifths below the melody line. Use both hands.
- Play the final line with thirds below but no fifths.
- Repeat the final line, playing the melody only at pitch and an octave lower.
- You can repeat it again just at pitch.
- If you have a swell box on your organ you might like to build a crescendo up to the third line and then down again during the fourth line and its repeat(s).

For another gentle improvisation

- Choose a tune.
- Choose similar registration to that above.
- Hold the tonic note (the key note) and the note five above it in the left hand in the octave between middle and tenor C.
- After a while, play the melody one octave higher than normal.
- You can make a pause between each line of the hymn, perhaps allowing just the left hand sounds to be heard.
- You might introduce thirds into one or two of the lines.
- As you reach the end of the melody, play the same fifth as you have been playing in the left hand, but now in the right hand and two octaves above the previous fifth.
- While you hold the fifth in the right hand, release it in the left hand and play the melody through again with your left hand.
- This can be particularly effective with hymns in minor keys.

A variant on the above

So far we have only changed the harmony of the music. Now try an experiment with the rhythm.

You could choose a similar registration, or even something a little louder.

- Begin as above with your fifth in the left hand.
- Let it sound for some while to establish itself.
- While continuing to hold the left hand, play the first line of the melody in the right hand but in short notes and not in time. You can play all the notes the same length, or some longer than others. If the original melody is in 4-time you might try it in 3-time.

You will probably need to practise getting the feel of doing this to a melody.

If you need a longer improvisation, repeat the process but with the melody an octave higher.

Another variant to try

- Begin by playing the melody in the lowest octave possible and with your left hand.
- You may prefer to play the printed rhythm, or you may wish to change it slightly.
- At the end of the first line, hold the last note with your left hand while you continue to play the second line of the melody with your right hand one octave higher.

- At the end of that line, hold the last note while you continue with the melody one octave higher in your left hand.
- Continue in this fashion to the end of the melody, or to the point when you run out of octaves.

You can then reverse the pattern as well, if you wish.

Another method to try

In preparation, try playing a scale in the key of your chosen hymn. Start on the key note, then play down to that note by descending from the octave above. You could try different rhythms like these, shown in the key of C, and many more of your own invention:

Choose one you like and that you think might go with your chosen hymn tune.

- Start by playing the scale passage.
- Then play the first line of the hymn. You might play it with all the usual harmony or just using thirds. You might play it in the original rhythm or change it in some way.
- Follow the first line with the scale passage again.
- Now play the second line of the hymn in the same style as the first line.
- Then the scale again, and so on.

You can experiment by playing lines in different octaves.

Another method to try

If you can play one pedal keyboard note, draw a gentle 16ft stop on the pedals and couple to your manual.

- Play the key note of the hymn on this pedal and hold it throughout.
- Above it, with your right hand play the hymn melody, preferably with a slightly altered rhythm. As an example, perhaps a 3-time melody could be played in 4-time, or vice versa.
- At the same time that you play the melody with your right hand, start your left hand on the same note as the pedal but one octave higher. Move it one note higher each bar.
- You might like to leave some breaks between melody lines of the hymn.

This method works really well if you reach the tonic note with the last line of the melody. You may be able to arrange that with a little trial and error starting on different notes.

And as a variant

Reverse the roles of the left and right hands in the above method. This is not quite as easy to accomplish as it sounds!

The joy of trying some of these ideas is that you cannot go wrong. There is no wrong. It is improvisation, and you will find that the spirit will take you sooner or later and you might well wonder at the result.